My First Bread Cookbook

For Kids of all Ages

No-knead bread
from the kitchen of
Artisan Bread with Steve

Updated 4.15.2022

By
Steve Gamelin

Copyright © 2016 by Steve Gamelin

All rights reserved. No part of this book may be used or reproduced, stored in a retrieval system, or transmitted in an form or by an means—electronics, mechanical, or any other—except for brief quotations in print reviews without prior permission of the author.

Now that I have met the standard legal requirements I would like to give my personal exceptions. I understand this is a cookbook and anyone who purchases this book can, (a) print and share the recipes with their friends, as you do with your other cookbooks (of course, it is my hope they too will start to make no-knead bread and buy my cookbooks) and (b) you may share a recipe or two on your website, etc. as long as you note the source and provide instructions on how your audience can acquire this book.
Thanks – Steve

Table of Contents

Letter from Steve 1

Overview & How to use this Cookbook 3

Ingredients 5

    Flour 5

    Salt 6

    Yeast 6

    Water 7

    Flavor Ingredients 7

Technique & Tips 8

    Prep 8

    Combining Ingredients 8

    1st Proofing (bulk fermentation) 8

    Degas, Pull & Stretch 10

    Roll-to-Coat 10

    Garnish & Baste 10

    Divide & Shape 10

    2nd Proofing 11

    Score 11

    Bake 11

    Storing Bread & Dough 12

    Equipment & Bakeware 12

    Impact of Weather on Bread Making 14

Guide to Bread Pans 15

"Traditional" No-Knead Bread Recipes ... proofs 8 to 12 hours 18

    Country White Bread (Basic "traditional" recipe & technique) 19

    Cheddar Cheese Bread (bread pan) 21

    Multigrain Country White Bread (bread pan) 23

    Honey Whole Wheat Bread (bread pan) 25

"Turbo" No-Knead Bread Recipes... ready to bake in 2-1/2 hours 27

    Country White Bread (Basic "Turbo" recipe & technique) 29

    Country White Bread (bread pan | garnished with sesame seeds) 31

    Multigrain Country White Bread (bread pan | garnished with oats) 33

Guide to Dutch Ovens & Long Covered Bakers 35

No-Knead Bread Recipes using Dutch Oven & Long Covered Baker 36

    Country White Bread (preheated cast iron Dutch oven) 37

    Harvest Grain Country White Bread (ceramic Dutch oven) 39

    Italian Sesame Seed Bread (long covered baker) 41

Guide to "Poor Man's Dutch Oven" (PMDO) 43

No-Knead Bread Recipes using a PMDO 45

    Country White Sandwich Bread (Basic PMDO recipe & technique) 45

    Honey Oatmeal Bread (PMDO... standard bread pans) 47

    Honey Whole Wheat Bread (PMDO... standard bread pans) 49

    Garlic Bread (PMDO... long bread pans) 51

    No-Knead Bread (PMDO... baked in a toaster oven) 53

Additional Bread Recipes 56

    Cheddar Cheese Bread (Dutch oven) 57

    Multigrain Whole Wheat Bread (PMDO) 59

- Harvest Grains Honey Whole Wheat Bread (Dutch oven) 61
- Sunflower Seed & Honey Whole Wheat (Dutch oven) 63
- Mediterranean Olive Bread (long covered baker | half loaves) 65
- Skillet Bread (skillet) 67

Rolls & Buns 70

- Easy Dinner Rolls ("Turbo" method | jumbo muffin pans) 71
- Pull-Apart Dinner Rolls (silicone baking pad) 73
- Garlic-Herb Rolls (mini round cake pans) 75
- Small Sandwich Rolls (mini loaf pans) 77
- Hamburger Buns (mini round cake pans) 79

No-Knead Pizza Dough & Pizza 81

- No-Knead Pizza Dough 82
  - "Traditional" Pizza Dough... proofs for 8 to 24 hours 83
  - "Turbo" Pizza Dough... proof for 1-1/2 hours 84
  - Personal Size Pizza Dough 85
- Mushroom-Black Olive Pizza 86
- Meatball & Bacon Pizza 87
- Perfect Little 9" Cheese Pizza 88
- Perfect Little 9" Mushroom-Black Olive Pizza 89
- Great Galloping Garlic Knots 90

Letter from Steve

The no-knead bread method has revolutionized bread baking. The average family can now have fresh from the oven bakery quality artisan bread in the convenience of their own home with little or no-kneading... Mother Nature does the kneading for you. No-yeast proofing... instant yeast does not need to be proofed in warm water prior to using. No mixer... ingredients can be combined with a spoon. It's almost as easy as making a bowl of *Campbell's* soup.

This is "New Age Bread Baking". I understand what Italian bread, French bread, and baguettes are, and I understand the proper techniques for making those breads, but we live in a new age and we should embrace new ideas. Instead of trying to emulate the bread methods of the past we should focus on our goal... to make great tasting, bakery quality, artisan bread with the methods and techniques that fit our busy schedules.

My Philosophy
I believe in "Smart & Easy". Note, I didn't say fast and cheap. I make no-knead bread because it's the smartest, easiest, way to make bakery quality artisan bread and I believe my readers and subscribers are attracted to the no-knead method for the same reasons. In response to my readers and subscribers, I strive for convenience and address each recipe from a very practical standpoint... as, I believe, they would want me to develop my recipes.

Smart: In the design of each recipe I try to be smart. I do my best to pick ingredients that are practical, reasonably priced, and easily available. I stay away from complex overlapping flavors and I use ingredients in moderation. More is not always better.

Easy: I look at each step in my recipes and try to simplify it. One of my most successful innovations was using an 8" skillet as a proofing basket. It shapes the dough during proofing and the handle makes it so easy to carry the dough to the baking vessel that even your kids could do it safely.

And I don't have a baker, food stylist or professional photographer... I baked the breads and took the pictures. My pictures are not as good as a professional photographer, but they accurately portray the results you can expect.

My Specialty
My specialty is to take the world's simplest list of ingredients (flour, salt, yeast and water) using the world's easiest bread making method (no mixer, no kneading, no yeast proofing) to create artisan breads that you would be proud to serve your family, friends and guests. One recipe, one method... with minor modifications I can make anything from a boule to an old-fashioned cinnamon roll.

I think you'll enjoy this cookbook.

Steve

If you want to impress a special friend,
or their parents,
make them a loaf of oven fresh bread.
And, if you have a science project due...
bake your teacher a loaf of bread.
Making bread is a science project.
You combine dry ingredients...
add wet ingredients...
let Mother Nature do her magic and
poof you have a loaf of bread.

Overview & How to use this Cookbook

This is the ideal bread cookbook for the newbie... the first timer... the future baker... because I will show you how to make bread in a glass bowl with a spoon... without dusting the counter with flour or touching the dough with your hands. It's called the "hands-free technique". It uses the principles of a bread machine... without the bread machine.

There are three basic methods for making bread...
- **Knead by hand...** the most common method.
- **Bread machine...** very popular, but your loaf will have a silly little paddle in the bottom.
- **No-knead...** a method in which Mother Nature does the kneading for you.

This cookbook uses the "no-knead" method. The advantages are...
- **No kneading...** Mother Nature does the kneading for you.
- **No yeast proofing...** instant yeast doesn't require proofing.
- **No special equipment (no mixer, no bread machine)...** entire process is done in a glass bowl with a spoon and spatula, and can be baked in a wide variety of baking vessels (bread pan, uncovered baker, skillet, preheated Dutch oven, etc.).

- **Only 4 ingredients (flour, salt, yeast and water)...** to which other ingredients can be added to make a variety of specialty breads.

There are two methods for making no-knead bread...
- **Traditional...** proofs for 8 to 24 hours.
- **"Turbo"...** ready to bake in 2-1/2 hours.

This cookbook will start by teaching you how to make no-knead bread using the traditional method, then "Turbo" method, because the traditional method is more popular and a little easier.

No-knead bread can be bake in a variety of baking vessels...
- **Bread pan...** the #1 baking vessel for bread
- **Dutch oven...** ideal for baking a round loaf (boule)
- **Long covered baker...** ideal for baking half loaves and long loaves.
- **Poor Man's Dutch Oven (PMDO)...** combines the ease of baking in a bread pan with the principles of baking in a Dutch oven.

This cookbook starts by showing you how to bake no-knead bread in a bread pan... it's easy and safer than working with a hot Dutch oven. Then we will expand our use of baking vessels to include the Dutch oven, covered baker, and "poor man's Dutch oven" (PMDO).

And we won't stop there. This cookbook will also show you how to make rolls, pizza, and pretzels..
- **Rolls...** you'll learn how to use bakeware to shape the rolls for you.
- **Pizza...** you'll learn how to make you own pizza dough.
- **Pretzels...** add one step to the process and you'll have pretzels.

What makes this cookbook different from others is...
- **"Hands-free technique"...** a new and innovative technique that uses the handle end of a plastic spoon to manipulate the dough (like a dough hook) after which the dough goes straight from the mixing bowl to the baking vessel (bread pan, etc.) without dusting the work surface with flour or touching the dough with your hands.
- **"Roll-to-coat"...** an innovative technique that coats the dough ball with flour in the mixing bowl. No more sticky dough. When the dough comes out of the bowl it will be easy to handle if you wish to divide the dough into portion to make baguettes, rolls, etc.
- **"Poor Man's Dutch Oven"...** new and innovative technique which combines the ease of baking in a bread pan with the principles of baking in a Dutch oven.

Step by step, this cookbook will take you on a journey you will love and enjoy.

Thanks - Steve

Ingredients

It only takes four ingredients to make bread... flour, salt, yeast and water.

Flour
Flour is the base ingredient of bread and there are four basic types of flour...

(1) <u>Bread flour</u> is designed for yeast bread. It has a higher percentage of gluten which gives artisan bread its airy crumb.

(2) <u>All-purpose flour</u> has less gluten than bread flour. I use all-purpose flour for biscuits, flatbreads, etc. In other words... I use it when I don't want an airy crumb.

(3) <u>Self-rising flour</u> is all-purpose flour with baking soda and baking powder added as leavening agents. It's intended for quick breads... premixed and ready to go. Do not use self-rising flour to make yeast bread. To see the difference between yeast and quick breads you may want to watch <u>No-Knead Artisan Beer Bread (updated)... super easy... no machines...</u> & <u>Introduction to Quick Beer Bread (a.k.a. Beer Bread Dinner Rolls)</u>.

(4) And there are a variety of <u>specialty flours</u>... whole wheat, rye, and a host of others. Each has its unique flavor and characteristics. In some cases, you can substitute specialty flour for bread flour, but you may need to tweak the recipe because most specialty flours have less gluten. I frequently blend specialty flour with bread flour.

Flour is the primary ingredient... if you don't use the correct flour you won't get the desired results.

Note: To know how many cups of flour there are in a specific bag... it's typically on the side in "Nutritional Facts". For example, this bag reads, "Serving Size 1/4 cup... Serving Per Container about 75". In other words... 18.75 (75 times 1/4). That's the technical answer, but in the real world (measuring cup versus weight) a bag of flour will measure differently based on density (sifted versus unsifted), type of flour (wheat is more dense than bread flour), humidity (flour weighs more on humid days), and all the other variables life and nature have to offer. Thus, there is no single correct answer, but for practical purposes... figure a 5 lb bag of bread flour is 17 to 18 cups.

Salt
While it is possible to make bread without salt... you would be disappointed. There are three basics types of salt...

(1) Most baking recipes are designed to use everyday table salt unless specified otherwise. Unless you're experienced, it is probably smartest to use table salt for your baking needs.

(2) Kosher salt is excellent. I use it when I cook, but a tablespoon of kosher salt does not equal a tablespoon of table salt because kosher salt crystals are larger.

(3) And, I use specialty salt as a garnish... for appearance and taste. For example, I use sea salt to garnish pretzels.

Generally speaking, when salt is added as an ingredient and baked it is difficult to taste the difference between table, kosher and sea salt. When salt is added as a garnish and comes in contact with the taste buds... kosher or specialty salt is an excellent choice.

Yeast
Yeast is the "magic" ingredient which transforms flour and water into dough. Traditional no-knead recipes use 1/4 tsp yeast (we want the dough to rise slowly which allows the dough to develop flavor). "Turbo" recipes use 1-1/4 tsp yeast (ready to bake in 2-1/2 hours). There are three basic types of yeast...

(1) The most common is active dry yeast which is traditionally proofed in warm water prior to being added to flour.

(2) Instant dry yeast (a.k.a. "instant yeast", "bread machine yeast", "quick rise", "rapid rise", "fast rising", etc.) which was designed for bread machines and does not need to be proofed in warm water... why worry about proofing yeast if you don't have too.

(3) Some older recipes call for <u>cake yeast</u> (a.k.a. "compressed yeast" or "fresh yeast"), but it's perishable. You can substitute active and instant dry yeast for cake yeast when using older recipes.

Update: While I respect the history of bread making and opinions of others, I do all my own testing. And, when I designed "Turbo" bread I found proofing technique was more important than the amount of yeast. In other words... when I proofed at 78 to 85 degrees F. it didn't make any difference if I use 1-1/4 or 2-1/4 ounces yeast... I got the same results. The reason is... the manufacturing of yeast has significantly improved yeast (more live yeast and better strains) since the 1940's when recipes called for a 2-1/4 ounce packet of yeast. When you bake a lot, you can save a lot by reducing the amount is yeast.

Furthermore, because the quality of dry yeast has improved... I now believe active dry yeast and instant yeast are interchangeable. Active dry yeast is a different stain of yeast (designed to act faster), but for all practical purposes the results is very similar.

Water
Water hydrates the ingredients and activates the yeast. The no-knead method uses a little more water than the typical recipe... and that's a good thing. It makes it easier to combine the wet and dry ingredients, and contributes to its airy crumb.

(1) I use <u>tap water</u>. It's convenient and easy, but sometimes city water has too much chlorine (chlorine kills yeast).

(2) If your dough does not rise during first proofing you may want to use <u>bottled drinking water</u>.

(3) But, do not use <u>distilled water</u> because the minerals have been removed.

Water is a flavor ingredient, if your water doesn't taste good... use bottled drinking water.

Flavor Ingredients
It only takes four ingredients to make bread... flour, salt, yeast and water, to which a variety of flavor ingredients can be added to make specialty breads such as... honey whole wheat, multigrain country white, rosemary, Mediterranean olive, cinnamon raisin, honey oatmeal, and a host of others.

Technique & Tips

The techniques used to make traditional and "Turbo" no-knead bread are identical except proofing. Turbo uses shorter proofing times, thus it is important to use sound proofing technique (warm ingredients and a warm proofing environment) when using the "Turbo" method. The traditional method is demonstrated on YouTube in No-Knead Bread 101 (Includes demonstration of Sesame Seed Bread... Italian, Muffuletta, & Sandwich). The "Turbo" method is demonstrated in Introduction to No-Knead "Turbo" Bread (updated)... ready to bake in 2-1/2 hours (super easy). And my complete collection of videos is available at http://nokneadbreadcentral.com/.

Prep
Traditional: Because the traditional method proof for 8 to 24 hours it uses cool water to slow the proofing process, thus the temperature of the bowl is not important.

Turbo: To insure consistency and assist Mother Nature with proofing... it's important to provide yeast with a warm proofing environment (78 to 85% F). One of the keys to proofing temperature is the temperature of the mixing bowl because it has direct contact with the dough. Thus, I run the bowl under warm water so that it doesn't draw the heat out of the warm water.

Combining Ingredients
Pour water in a 3 to 4 qt glass mixing bowl (use warm water and a warm bowl for "Turbo" and cool for traditional). Add salt, yeast, flavor ingredients, etc... and stir to combine (it will insure the ingredients are evenly distributed). Add flour (flour will resist the water and float). Start by stirring the ingredients with the handle end of a plastic spoon drawing the flour from the sides into the middle of bowl (vigorously mixing will not hydrate the flour faster... but it will raise a lot of dust). Within 30 seconds the flour will hydrate and form a shaggy ball. Then scrape dry flour from side of bowl and tumble dough to combine moist flour with dry flour (about 15 seconds). It takes about one minute to combine wet and dry ingredients.

Traditional: Cover bowl with plastic wrap, place on counter, and proof for 8 to 24 hours.

Turbo: Cover bowl with plastic wrap, place in a warm draft free location, and proof for 1-1/2 hours.

1st Proofing (bulk fermentation)
The process is called "proofing" because it "proves" the yeast is active.

Bread making is nature at work (yeast is a living organism) and subject to nature. Seasons (summer vs. winter) and weather (heat & humidity) have a direct impact on proofing. In other words, don't worry if your dough varies in size... that's Mother Nature. Just focus on your goal... if the gluten forms (dough develops a stringy nature) and doubles in size... you're good to go.

If your dough does <u>not</u> rise the usual culprits are... outdated yeast or chlorinated water (chlorine kills yeast). Solution, get fresh yeast and/or use bottled drinking water.

If your dough is <u>slow</u> (takes "forever") to rise... your proofing temperature is probably too cool.

Traditional: Because the traditional method use long proofing times (8 to 24 hours) it does not require any special technique.

Turbo: Because "Turbo" dough use shorter proofing times (1-12/ hours) it is important to practice sound proofing technique.

The ideal temperature for proofing is 78 to 85 degrees F, but the typically home is 68 to 72 degrees, which is why recipes generally suggest proofing in a "warm draft-free environment". So, you have a choice... wait longer or create a warm proofing environment. My favorites are...

Oven setting: If your oven has a setting for proofing (80 degrees F)... use it.

Direct sunlight: Cover bowl with plastic wrap, place in direct sunlight, and the heat from the Sun will create a favorable proofing environment.

Oven light: If your oven has a light... cover bowl with plastic wrap, place in oven, turn light on, and close the door. The oven light will generate heat and increase the temperature inside the oven by several degrees. The amount of heat will depend on the size of the oven and strength of the bulb. The oven temperature will always start low and climb slowly, but it may go over 90 degrees F. so check periodically until you are familiar with the nature of your oven.

Desk Lamp: Cover bowl with plastic wrap, place under a desk lamp, lower lamp so that it's close to the bowl, and turn lamp on. The plastic wrap over the bowl will create a similar effect to leaving car windows rolled up on a sunny day.

Microwave: Place an 8 to 16 oz cup of water in the microwave and heat on high for 2 minutes. Then move the cup to the back corner, place mixing bowl (dough) in microwave and close the door. The heat and steam from the hot water will create a favorable environment for proofing.

Folding dough proofer: Commercial bakeries have large proofing ovens in which they can control climate and temperature. There are smaller versions available for the public that fold flat.

Tip: To fit bread making into your schedule... you can extend 1st proofing up to 4 hours (or even more), but don't shorten... it important to give Mother Nature time to form the gluten.

Degas, Pull & Stretch
The purpose of degassing, pulling and stretching is to, (a) expel the gases that formed during bulk fermentation, (b) strengthen the dough by realigning and stretching the gluten strands, and (c) stimulate yeast activity for 2nd proofing.

Because no-knead dough is sticky and difficult to handle... I degas, pull & stretch dough by stirring it in the bowl with the handle end of a plastic spoon (like a dough hook). It will reduce the size of the dough ball by 50% making it easier to handle and the process replaces folding and shaping in most cases.

Roll-to-Coat
Before removing the dough from bowl... dust the dough and side of the bowl with flour, then roll-to-coat. The flour will bond to the sticky dough making it easier to handle, but do not roll-to-coat with flour if you're going to garnish or baste.

Garnish & Baste
The purpose of garnishing and basting is to enhance the appearance of the crust, but it isn't necessary. If you decide to garnish and baste there are two techniques... roll-to-coat and skillet method.

Roll-to-Coat Method: Before removing dough from bowl... add ingredients to bowl (on the dough and side of the bowl), then roll to coat. For example, when I garnish honey oatmeal bread... I sprinkle oat in the bowl and on the dough, then roll the dough ball in the oats and they will bond to the sticky dough. This can also be done with seeds, grains, olive oil, egg wash, etc.

Skillet Method: When I want to garnish and/or baste the top of the loaf... I coat the proofing skillet with baste (egg wash, olive oil, vegetable oil, etc.) and sprinkle with the garnish (oats, seeds, grains, etc.). The ingredients will bond with the dough as the dough proofs.

Supporting video: <u>How to Garnish & Baste No-Knead Bread using "Hands-Free" Technique</u>

Divide & Shape
If you're not going to divide the dough... it can go straight from the mixing bowl to the proofing skillet or baking vessel. If you are going to divide and shape the dough... dust the dough and side of the bowl with flour and roll-to-coat, dust work surface with flour, roll the dough ball out of the bowl (excess flour and all) onto the work surface, and divide and shape. I use a plastic bowl scraper to

assist in dividing, shaping and carry the dough to the baking vessel. Together they (flour & bowl scraper) make it easier to handle the dough.

2nd Proofing

Traditional: Originally I proofed for 1 to 2 hours, but over time I have been baking more in bread pans and found shorter proofing times gave better results. I now proof for 30 to 60 minutes.

Turbo: Place dough in a warm draft-free location and proof for 30 minutes.

Tip: To fit bread making into your schedule... you can extend 2nd proofing times, but you don't want the dough to exceed the size of the baking vessel. If you're using a large baking vessel (Dutch oven, etc.) it's never a problem, but if you're using a bread pan don't allow the dough to exceed the sides of the pan before baking or your loaf will droop over the sides and be less attractive. But, always bake it... it will still be delicious.

Score

The purpose of scoring dough is to provide seams to control where the crust will split during "oven spring", but it isn't necessary to score dough. If you do decide to score your loaf you may want to use a scissors (no-knead dough is very moist and more likely to stretch than slice). Personally, I place the dough in the baking vessel seam side up... the dough will split at the seam during "oven spring" which gives the loaf a nice rustic appearance.

Bake

Baking Time: Bread is done when it reaches an internal temperature of 185 to 220 degrees F. and the crumb (inside of the bread) isn't doughy. Baking times in my recipes are designed to give bread an internal temperature of 200 to 205 degrees F, but ovens vary and you may need to adjust your baking times slightly.

No-Stick Spray: Most bakeware has a non-stick surface, but it is safest to spray your bakeware unless you are fully confident your bread won't stick.

Ovens: Ovens aren't always accurate. I check the temperature of ovens and bakeware. Ovens with a digital readout that displays the temperature as they preheat are typically very accurate, but ovens that say they will be at temperature in a specific number of minutes are not always accurate. My point is... you will get the best results if you learn the character and nature of your oven.

Oven Rack: Generally speaking you want to bake bread and rolls in the middle or lower third of the oven, but it isn't critical. Just keep them away from the upper heating element or they may brown a little too quickly.

Oven Spring: When dough is first put into the oven it will increase in size by as much as a third in a matter of minutes because, (a) gases trapped in the dough will expand, (b) moisture will turn into steam and try to push its way out, and (c) yeast will become highly active converting sugars into gases. The steam and gases work together to create "oven spring". Once the internal temperature of the bread reaches 120 degrees F... the yeast will begin to die and the crust will harden.

Storing Bread & Dough
After allowing bread to cool... it can be wrapped in plastic wrap, or stored in a zip-lock plastic bag, or plastic bread bags (available on the web). If you wish to keep bread for a longer period of time... slice it into portions and freeze them in a zip-lock freezer bag (remove excess air). Do not store bread in the refrigerator. Bread goes stale faster in the refrigerator.

If you wish to save dough... divide it into portions, drizzle each portion with olive oil, place in zip-lock bag, remove excess air, and refrigerate for up to two days or freeze for up to two months. To thaw dough... move dough from freezer to refrigerator the day before (12 or more hours), then place on counter for 30 minutes before use to come to room temperature.

Equipment & Bakeware
Bowl for Mixing: You can use any 3 to 4 qt bowl. I use a 3-1/2 qt glass bowl because, (a) there's ample room for the dough to expand, (b) plastic wrap sticks to glass, and (c) I don't want the rim of my bowl to exceed the width of the plastic wrap.

Measuring Spoons: I'm sure you already have measuring spoons in the kitchen... they will work just fine. If you're going to buy new, I prefer oval versus round because an oval shape will fit into jars and containers more easily.

Measuring Cups: Dry measuring cups are designed to be filled to the top and leveled. Liquid measuring cups have a pour spout and are designed to be filled to the gradations on the side (neither measures weight). It is best to use the appropriate measuring cup.

Note: U.S. and metric measuring cups may be used interchangeably... there is only a slight difference (±3%). More importantly, the ingredients of a recipe measured with a set (U.S. or metric) will have their volumes in the same proportion to one another.

Spoon for Combining Wet and Dry Ingredients: A spoon is an excellent tool for combining wet and dry ingredients. Surprisingly, I found the handle end of a plastic spoon worked best for me because, I didn't have a big clump on the end like some of my other mixing utensils (which makes it easier to stir and manipulate the dough). And when you think about it... mixers don't use a paddle to mix dough, they use a hook which looks a lot like the handle end of my spoon.

Silicon Baking Mat: Silicone baking mats are very useful... I use them as reusable parchment paper (they're environmentally friendly). Silicone baking mats serve two purposes... (a) as a work surface for folding and shaping (they have excellent non-stick properties), and (b) as a baking mat... specifically when the dough is difficult to move after folding and shaping. And I slide a cookie sheet under the mat before baking (it makes it easier to put the mat into and take it out of the oven).

Spatula: I use a spatula to scrape the sides of the bowl to get the last bits of flour incorporated into the dough.

Plastic Bowl Scraper: I use a plastic bowl scraper verses a metal dough scraper because it's the better multi-tasker. I use the bowl scraper to (a) fold, shape, and divide the dough, (b) assist in transporting the dough to the proofing vessel, (c) scrape excess flour off the work surface, (d) scrape excess flour out of the bowl (after all it is a bowl scraper), and (e) scrape any remaining bits in the sink towards the disposal. It's a useful multi-tasker and you can't do all those tasks with a metal cough scraper.

Timer: I'm sure you already have a timer and it will work just fine. If you're thinking about a new one... I prefer digital because they're more accurate.

Proofing Baskets & Vessels: The purpose of a proofing basket or vessel is to pre-shape the dough prior to baking (dough will spread if it isn't contained). Because no-knead dough has a tendency to stick to the lining of proofing baskets... I use common household items as proofing vessels. For example, I use an 8" skillet (with no-stick spray) to pre-shape dough when baking in a Dutch oven. It shapes the dough during proofing, and the handle makes it easy to carry the dough and put it in the hot Dutch oven safely.

You can also proof dough in the baking vessel if it doesn't have to be preheated. For example, standard loaves are typically proof and baked in the bread pan where your bread pan shapes the loaf during proofing and baking. You can use this same principle for shaping and baking rolls and buns.

Baking Vessels: Baking vessels come in a variety of sizes, shapes and materials. You can change the appearance of the loaf by sampling changing the baking vessel.

Plastic Wrap & Proofing Towel: I use plastic wrap for 1st proofing and a lint-free towel for 2nd proofing. Plastic wrap protects dough for longer proofing times and can be used to create a favorable proofing environment (solar effect).

Cooling Rack: The purpose of a cooling rack is to expose the bottom of the loaf during the cooling process.

Bread Bags: I use plastic bread bags to store bread after they have cooled. And they're great for packaging bread as gifts. I also use paper bags as gifts when the loaf is still warm and I don't want to trap the moisture in a plastic bag... it gives a nice natural appearance.

10" Flat Whisk: I use a flat whisk to combine dry ingredients with yogurt... a flat whisk will slice through yogurt forming small clump. If you use a balloon whisk a big lump will form inside the balloon.

Pastry/Pizza Roller: When you watch shows they hand shape and toss pizza dough, but I find it more practical to use a pastry/pizza roller. It is also useful when shaping flatbread and cinnamon rolls.

Impact of Weather on Bread Making

Elevations: Higher elevations have lower air pressure. As a result, yeast creates larger bubbles and the dough rises too fast... before properly developing flavor and texture. Solution, proof in a cool location or refrigerator to slow fermentation. Higher elevations will also cause dehydration, but that usually isn't a problem because no-knead dough has a high moisture content.

Humidity: Low humidity makes ingredients dryer and high humidity adds moisture to ingredients (especially flour). Fortunately bread making is very forgiving, but there are times you will want to make minor adjustments. For example, on cold winter days with low humidity you may want to add 1 to 2 ounces of water if the dough is dryer than normal. For high humidity, I have never found it necessary to reduce the amount of water, because I can always "roll-to-coat" the dough in flour to make it easier to handle.

Temperature: The ideal temperature for proofing dough is 78 to 85 degrees F. Dough takes longer to proof in cooler temperatures (77 degrees and lower) and dough proofs faster in warm temperatures (86 degrees and higher). Thus, when the house is cold I extend the proofing time from 8 to 24 hours using the "traditional" method. And, I use the "oven light method" of proofing to create a warm draft free environment for proofing when using the "Turbo" method. When the house is warm, you can start any time the dough is ready.

Guide to Bread Pans

When I decided to bake no-knead bread in a bread pan, I felt it was important to test the options. Nothing earth-shaking, but a little general discussion may help you select the best pan for your intended purpose.

Basic Loaf Sizes
Loafs vary in size... some folks like larger loafs... some like smaller. No right... no wrong... it's personal taste. I like to use one pound of flour. A five pound bag of flour is typically 17 & 1/2 cups (3-1/2 cups per pound), which is why most of the recipes in this cookbook use 3-1/2 cups flour.

Basic Pan Sizes
Small (8" x 4"): Raisin bread is typically smaller than the other loaves. As a result, I use 3 cups flour (versus 3-1/2) and a smaller bread pan.

Medium (8-1/2" x 4-1/2") and Large (9" x 5"): These are the two most popular size bread pans. They are interchangeable... you can use either for all the recipes in this cookbook. The medium size loaf pan will give you a little taller loaf and the large will give you a little wider loaf.

Extra Large (9-1/2" x 5-1/2"): You may want to use 4 to 5 cups flour when baking in an extra large loaf pan.

Long (12" x 4-1/2"): The long bread pan is ideally suited for making long and half loaves.

Bottom-line: The medium (8-1/2" x 4-1/2") and large (9" x 5") bread pans are ideally suited for a one pound loaf (3-1/2 cups flour).

Types of Bread Pans
The type of bread pan you use can make a difference.

Standard Metal Bread Pans: Standard metal loaf pans are the most popular... they're inexpensive and perform well. In my tests they all preformed equally well (internal temperatures were all very similar after baking) except the thin super cheap one.

Cast Iron: It's fun to bake with cast iron and it will give you an excellent loaf, but they are more expensive and the taste tasters couldn't tell the difference.

Stoneware: Frequently we associate loaf pans with bread, but loaf pans are designed for a variety of uses (casseroles, meatloaf, etc.). I am very attracted to stoneware when I bake & serve in them... they look terrific, but they bake slower (take longer to heat) and they give bread a soft bottom.

Glass: Glass loaf pans brake, take longer to heat, and gives bread a soft bottom.

Unique: I included a 9" pie pan in the picture to make a point... you can bake bread in anything from a bread pan to a pie pan or skillet.

Overview
Metal bread pans: Metal pans were the clear winner. They heat faster and did an excellent job baking the crumb and developing the crust.

Heavy loaf pans: Loaf pans made of stoneware and glass did not fare as well. The internal temperature was 200+ degrees F (like the others), but the crust did not develop as well and the top had a tendency to sag.

Shape: I like pans with handles and rounded corners... the handles make them easier to take out of the oven and the rounded corners are easier to clean.

Note: When shopping for bread pans, you may want to buy 2 matching pans as discussed in Guide to "Poor Man's Dutch Oven".

Author's Note

The traditional method for making no-knead bread
uses 3 cups flour and was designed to be baked in a Dutch oven.

When I developed no-knead "Turbo" bread
I designed it to be baked in a bread pan
which uses 3-1/2 cups flour
(loaves using 3 cups flour are
too small for a standard bread pan).

Because I wanted the flexibility of using
any recipe with any baking technique...
I converted the majority of my recipes to 3-1/2 cups flour.

After all, you can always use 3-1/2 cups flour
to make a boule in a Dutch oven,
but you can't use 3 cups flour to make a standard loaf.

<<<<([|])>>>>

Large Loaf Option

It should also be noted...
you can adjust the size of any of my recipes
to fit larger baking vessels by
adding 2 oz more water, 1/2 cup more flour
(all other ingredients remain the same),
and increase baking time by 5 minutes.
As demonstrated in...
How to Adjust Loaf Size to Larger Pans

"Traditional" No-Knead Bread Recipes ... proofs 8 to 12 hours

There are two methods for making no-knead bread... "Traditional" (proofs for 8 to 24 hours) and "Turbo" (ready to bake in 2-1/2 hours). We'll start with the traditional because it is easier and more popular.

If you aren't familiar with my recipes and technique... you may want to watch: [No-Knead Bread 101 (Includes demonstration of Sesame Seed Bread... Italian, Muffuletta, & Sandwich)](#).

Country White Bread (Basic "traditional" recipe & technique)
I picked this recipe to be your first loaf because it's the easiest... it has the fewest steps and it's baked in a bread pan. Here's how simple it is... combine ingredients in a glass bowl, mix with the handle end of a plastic spoon, cover with plastic wrap, and leave it on the counter to proof over night and it will be ready to bake in the morning at which time you will... spray a bread pan with no-stick spray, roll the dough out of the bowl into the pan, proof for 30 minutes, and bake. Simple, easy, fun.

What's new: This is the basic recipe using "hands-free technique". With minor changes in the following recipes you will be able to make a variety of breads.

Supporting video: World's Easiest No-Knead Bread (Introducing "Hands-Free" Technique)

Country White Bread

Pour water into a 3 to 4 qt glass mixing bowl.

    14 oz cool Water

Add salt and yeast... give a quick stir to combine.

    1-1/2 tsp Salt
    1/4 tsp Dry Yeast (Instant or Active Dry Yeast)

Add flour... stir until dough forms a shaggy ball, scrape dry flour from side of bowl, then tumble dough to combine moist flour with dry flour.

    3-1/2 cups Bread Flour

Cover bowl with plastic wrap, place on counter, and proof for 8 to 24 hours.

8 to 24 hours later (bread pan)

When dough has risen and developed its gluten structure... spray the bread pan (8-1/2" x 4-1/2" or 9" x 5") with no-stick cooking spray and set aside.

"Degas, pull and stretch"... stick handle end of a plastic spoon in the dough and stir (dough will form a sticky ball). Then, scrape side of bowl to get remainder of the dough into the sticky dough ball.

Roll dough out of bowl into bread pan.

Place pan in a warm draft-free location, cover with a lint-free towel, and proof for 30 minutes.

Before dough is fully proofed...

Adjust oven rack so that the bread will be in the middle of the oven and pre-heat to 400 degrees F.

30 minutes later

When the dough has proofed and oven has come to temperature... place loaf pan in the oven and bake for 40 minutes.

40 minutes later

Remove bread pan from oven, gently turn loaf out on work surface and place on cooling rack.

Poof... you made your first no-knead bread.

Cheddar Cheese Bread (bread pan)

This is a gorgeous loaf and it's easy to make… just add cheese. It's something your parents and friends will love.

What's new: This recipe adds a flavor ingredient (cheese)… how simple is that. Flavor ingredients are added to either the wet or dry ingredients, depending on the nature of the flavor ingredient you're adding. And note, I used <u>coarsely</u> shredded Cheddar Cheese to create the speckled effect. Also note, the water was increased to compensate for the cheese.

Cheddar Cheese Bread

Pour water into a 3 to 4 qt glass mixing bowl.
> 16 oz cool Water

Add salt and yeast... give a quick stir to combine.
> 1-1/2 tsp Salt
> 1/4 tsp Dry Yeast (Instant or Active Dry Yeast)

Add flour... then add cheese on top of the flour (if cheese is added before flour it will be harder to combine)... stir until dough forms a shaggy ball, scrape dry flour from side of bowl, then tumble dough to combine moist flour with dry flour.
> 3-1/2 cups Bread Flour
> 1 cup coarsely shredded Cheddar Cheese

Cover bowl with plastic wrap, place on counter, and proof for 8 to 24 hours.

8 to 24 hours later (bread pan)

When dough has risen and developed its gluten structure... spray the bread pan (8-1/2" x 4-1/2" or 9" x 5") with no-stick cooking spray and set aside.

"Degas, pull and stretch"... stick handle end of a plastic spoon in the dough and stir (dough will form a sticky ball). Then, scrape side of bowl to get remainder of the dough into the sticky dough ball.

Roll dough out of bowl into bread pan.

Place pan in a warm draft-free location, cover with a lint-free towel, and proof for 30 minutes.

Before dough is fully proofed...

Adjust oven rack so that the bread will be in the middle of the oven and pre-heat to 400 degrees F.

30 minutes later

When the dough has proofed and oven has come to temperature... place loaf pan in the oven and bake for 40 minutes.

40 minutes later

Remove bread pan from oven, gently turn loaf out on work surface and place on cooling rack.

Multigrain Country White Bread (bread pan)

This is one of my most popular loaves. My first multigrain loaves used 2 cups bread flour and 1 cup wheat flour. One time I forgot the wheat flour and used 3 cups bread flour. Surprise, surprise... the multigrain country white became one of my most popular breads. I had assumed those who liked grains also liked wheat breads, but there appears to be a significant segment of our society who likes multigrain bread without the wheat bread taste. Wheat is one of those things you either like or don't like, but it doesn't mean you don't like multigrain bread.

What's new: This recipe adds seeds and oats. The seeds are added to the wet ingredients and stirred to evenly distribute them. The oats are added on top of the dry ingredients to prevent them from absorbing the water before the flour. And note, the water was increased to compensate for the oats.

Multigrain Country White Bread

Pour water into a 3 to 4 qt glass mixing bowl.
> 16 oz cool Water

Add salt, yeast, and seeds... give a quick stir to combine.
> 1-1/2 tsp Salt
> 1/4 tsp Dry Yeast (Instant or Active Dry Yeast)
> 1 Tbsp Sesame Seeds
> 1 Tbsp Flax Seeds

Add flour... then add oats on top of the flour (if oats are added before flour they will absorb the water and it will be harder to combine)... stir until dough forms a shaggy ball, scrape dry flour from side of bowl, then tumble dough to combine moist flour with dry flour.
> 3-1/2 cups Bread Flour
> 1/2 cup Old Fashioned *Quaker* Oats

Cover bowl with plastic wrap, place on counter, and proof for 8 to 24 hours.

8 to 24 hours later (bread pan)

When dough has risen and developed its gluten structure... spray the bread pan (8-1/2" x 4-1/2" or 9" x 5") with no-stick cooking spray and set aside.

"Degas, pull and stretch"... stick handle end of a plastic spoon in the dough and stir (dough will form a sticky ball). Then, scrape side of bowl to get remainder of the dough into the sticky dough ball.

Roll dough out of bowl into bread pan.

Place pan in a warm draft-free location, cover with a lint-free towel, and proof for 30 minutes.

Before dough is fully proofed...

Adjust oven rack so that the bread will be in the middle of the oven and pre-heat to 400 degrees F.

30 minutes later

When the dough has proofed and oven has come to temperature... place loaf pan in the oven and bake for 40 minutes.

40 minutes later

Remove bread pan from oven, gently turn loaf out on work surface and place on cooling rack.

Honey Whole Wheat Bread (bread pan)

This recipe combines whole wheat flour with bread flour, which gives you the nutrition and nutty taste of whole wheat with the crumb of a Country White in a hearty loaf with a touch of honey for sweetness.

What's new: This recipe adds two flavor ingredients, olive oil and honey. They are added to the wet ingredients and stirred to combine. Then whole wheat flour is combined with bread flour to make your first wheat bread. The blending of flours will give the loaf a crumb (the inside of the bread).

Note: Make sure your wheat four is fresh (less than 6 months old) because whole wheat flour contains wheat germ... therefore oils... and the oils can make the flour rancid (not good eats) after six months.

Honey Whole Wheat Bread

Pour water into a 3 to 4 qt glass mixing bowl.
> 16 oz cool Water

Add salt, yeast, olive oil and honey... give a quick stir to combine.
> 1-1/2 tsp Salt
> 1/4 tsp Dry Yeast (Instant or Active Dry Yeast)
> 1 Tbsp extra-virgin Olive Oil
> 1 Tbsp Honey

Add flour... stir until dough forms a shaggy ball, scrape dry flour from side of bowl, then tumble dough to combine moist flour with dry flour.
> 2 cups Bread Flour
> 1-1/2 cups Whole Wheat Flour

Cover bowl with plastic wrap, place on counter, and proof for 8 to 24 hours.

8 to 24 hours later (bread pan)

When dough has risen and developed its gluten structure... spray the bread pan (8-1/2" x 4-1/2" or 9" x 5") with no-stick cooking spray and set aside.

"Degas, pull and stretch"... stick handle end of a plastic spoon in the dough and stir (dough will form a sticky ball). Then, scrape side of bowl to get remainder of the dough into the sticky dough ball.

Roll dough out of bowl into bread pan.

Place pan in a warm draft-free location, cover with a lint-free towel, and proof for 30 minutes.

Before dough is fully proofed...

Adjust oven rack so that the bread will be in the middle of the oven and pre-heat to 400 degrees F.

30 minutes later

When the dough has proofed and oven has come to temperature... place loaf pan in the oven and bake for 40 minutes.

40 minutes later

Remove bread pan from oven, gently turn loaf out on work surface and place on cooling rack.

"Turbo" No-Knead Bread Recipes... ready to bake in 2-1/2 hours

Now that you have mastered traditional no-knead bread... it's time to learn how to make no-knead bread that will be ready to bake in 2-1/2 hours. It was designed for those who want to make no-knead bread, but... don't want to wait 8 to 24 hours. For those who want bread machine bread, but... don't want to buy and store a bread machine.

There are two changes... ingredients and sound proofing technique.

Ingredients
Yeast is the active ingredient that makes the dough rise, thus shorter proofing times require more yeast. As a result, the recipe calls for 1-1/4 teaspoons yeast.

Sound proofing technique
Use a warm bowl, warm ingredients and warm proofing environment. The ideal temperature for proofing is 78 to 85 degrees F, but the typically home is 68 to 72 degrees, which is why recipes generally suggest proofing in a "warm draft-free environment". So, you have a choice... wait longer for the dough to proof or create a warm proofing environment. My favorite techniques for creating a warm proofing environment are...

Oven setting: If your oven has a setting for proofing (80 degrees F)... use it.

Direct sunlight: Cover bowl with plastic wrap, place in direct sunlight, and the heat from the Sun will create a more favorable proofing environment.

Oven light: If your oven has a light... cover bowl with plastic wrap, place in oven, turn light on, and close the door. The oven light will generate heat and increase the temperature inside the oven by several degrees. The amount of heat will depend on the size of the oven and strength of the bulb. The oven temperature will start low and climb slowly. Each oven is different, so check periodically until you are familiar with the nature of your oven.

Desk Lamp: Cover bowl with plastic wrap, place under a desk lamp, lower lamp so that it's close to the bowl, and turn lamp on. The plastic wrap over the bowl will create a similar effect to leaving car windows rolled up on a sunny day.

Supporting video: Introduction to No-Knead "Turbo" Bread (updated)... ready to bake in 2-1/2 hours (super easy) | How to Proof Bread Dough (a.k.a. The Dynamics of Proofing)

Country White Bread (Basic "Turbo" recipe & technique)
This is the same loaf as the traditional Country White Bread using the "Turbo" method (ingredients & technique). They will look and taste the same.

What's new: This recipe shows you how to make no-knead bread in less time... 2-1/2 hours verses 8 to 24 hours. Three things... (a) use a warm bowl and warm ingredients (warm temperatures encourage yeast activity), (b) use 1-1/4 tsp yeast verses 1/4 tsp yeast (shorter proofing times need additional yeast), and (c) it very important to proof in a warm, draft-free, environment (78 to 85 degrees).

Important note: You can apply the "Turbo" technique to any of my recipes. The ingredients are independent of the method.

Country White Bread... ready to bake in 2-1/2 hours

Pour warm water in a 3 to 4 qt warm glass mixing bowl (use a warm bowl... you don't want a cold bowl to take the heat out of the warm water).

>14 oz warm Water

Add salt and yeast... give a quick stir to combine.

>1-1/2 tsp Salt
>1-1/4 tsp Dry Yeast (Instant or Active Dry Yeast)

Add flour... stir until dough forms a shaggy ball, scrape dry flour from side of bowl, then tumble dough to combine moist flour with dry flour.

>3-1/2 cups Bread Flour

Cover bowl with plastic wrap, place in a warm draft-free location, and proof for 1-1/2 hours.

1-1/2 hours later (bread pan)

When dough has risen and developed its gluten structure... spray the bread pan (8-1/2" x 4-1/2" or 9" x 5") with no-stick cooking spray and set aside.

"Degas, pull and stretch"... stick handle end of a plastic spoon in the dough and stir (dough will form a sticky ball). Then, scrape side of bowl to get remainder of the dough into the sticky dough ball.

Roll dough out of bowl into bread pan.

Place pan in a warm draft-free location, cover with a lint-free towel, and proof for 30 minutes.

Before dough is fully proofed...

Adjust oven rack so that the bread will be in the middle of the oven and pre-heat to 400 degrees F.

30 minutes later

When the dough has proofed and oven has come to temperature... place loaf pan in the oven and bake for 40 minutes.

40 minutes later

Remove bread pan from oven, gently turn loaf out on work surface and place on cooling rack.

Country White Bread (bread pan | garnished with sesame seeds)
Garnishing a loaf with sesame seeds is easy and it gives the loaf a special appearance.

What's new: This recipe demonstrates how to use the "roll-to-coat" technique to garnish the crust.

No-knead dough is very sticky... this techniques takes advantage of the sticky dough. After proofing... (a) stick the handle end of the plastic spoon in the dough and stir (the dough will form a sticky ball), (b) scrape the side of the bowl to get the remainder of the dough into the sticky dough ball, then (c) sprinkle 2 Tbsp of sesame seeds on the dough ball and side of the bowl, and use the spoon handle to roll the dough in the seeds (the seeds will bond to the sticky dough). Poof, you've garnished your loaf with sesame seeds.

Country White Bread garnished with sesame seeds

Pour warm water in a 3 to 4 qt warm glass mixing bowl (use a warm bowl... you don't want a cold bowl to take the heat out of the warm water).

> 14 oz warm Water

Add salt and yeast... give a quick stir to combine.

> 1-1/2 tsp Salt
> 1-1/4 tsp Dry Yeast (Instant or Active Dry Yeast)

Add flour... stir until dough forms a shaggy ball, scrape dry flour from side of bowl, then tumble dough to combine moist flour with dry flour.

> 3-1/2 cups Bread Flour

Cover bowl with plastic wrap, place in a warm draft-free location, and proof for 1-1/2 hours.

1-1/2 hours later (bread pan | garnish)

When dough has risen and developed its gluten structure... spray the bread pan (8-1/2" x 4-1/2" or 9" x 5") with no-stick cooking spray and set aside.

"Degas, pull and stretch"... stick handle end of a plastic spoon in the dough and stir (dough will form a sticky ball). Then, scrape side of bowl to get remainder of the dough into the sticky dough ball.

Garnish... sprinkle dough ball and side of bowl with sesame seeds and roll-to-coat (roll dough ball in sesame seeds to coat).

> 2 Tbsp Sesame Seeds

Roll dough out of bowl into bread pan.

Place pan in a warm draft-free location, cover with a lint-free towel, and proof for 30 minutes.

Before dough is fully proofed...

Adjust oven rack so that the bread will be in the middle of the oven and pre-heat to 400 degrees F.

30 minutes later

When the dough has proofed and oven has come to temperature... place loaf pan in the oven and bake for 40 minutes.

40 minutes later

Remove bread pan from oven, gently turn loaf out on work surface and place on cooling rack.

Multigrain Country White Bread (bread pan | garnished with oats)
Wow, this is a gorgeous loaf with flavor to match. It's hard to believe it was made in a glass bowl with a spoon.

What's new: This recipe adds seeds to the wet ingredients, oats to the dry ingredients (just like Multigrain Country White Bread), then it's garnished with oats. To garnish... (a) stick the handle end of the plastic spoon in the dough and stir (dough will form a sticky ball), (b) scrape the side of the bowl to get the remainder of the dough into the sticky dough ball, (c) sprinkle 1/4 cup Old Fashioned *Quaker* Oats on the dough ball and side of the bowl, then use the spoon handle to roll the dough in the oats. It's that simple.

Multigrain Country White Bread

Pour warm water in a 3 to 4 qt warm glass mixing bowl (use a warm bowl... you don't want a cold bowl to take the heat out of the warm water).

 16 oz warm Water

Add salt, yeast and seeds... give a quick stir to combine.

 1-1/2 tsp Salt
 1-1/4 tsp Dry Yeast (Instant or Active Dry Yeast)
 1 Tbsp Sesame Seeds
 1 Tbsp Flax Seeds

Add flour... then oats (if oats are added before flour they will absorb the water and it will be harder to combine)... stir until dough forms a shaggy ball, scrape dry flour from side of bowl, then tumble dough to combine moist flour with dry flour.

 3-1/2 cups Bread Flour
 1/2 cup Old Fashioned *Quaker* Oats

Cover bowl with plastic wrap, place in a warm draft-free location, and proof for 1-1/2 hours.

1-1/2 hours later (bread pan | garnish)

When dough has risen and developed its gluten structure... spray the bread pan (8-1/2" x 4-1/2" or 9" x 5") with no-stick cooking spray and set aside.

"Degas, pull and stretch"... stick handle end of a plastic spoon in the dough and stir (dough will form a sticky ball). Then, scrape side of bowl to get remainder of the dough into the sticky dough ball.

Garnish... sprinkle dough ball and side of bowl with oats, and roll-to-coat (roll dough ball in oats to coat).

 1/4 cup Old Fashioned *Quaker* Oats

Roll dough out of bowl into bread pan.

Place pan in a warm draft-free location, cover with a lint-free towel, and proof for 30 minutes.

Before dough is fully proofed...

Adjust oven rack so that the bread will be in the middle of the oven and pre-heat to 400 degrees F.

30 minutes later

When the dough has proofed and oven has come to temperature... place loaf pan in the oven and bake for 40 minutes.

40 minutes later

Remove bread pan from oven, gently turn loaf out on work surface and place on cooling rack.

Guide to Dutch Ovens & Long Covered Bakers

The purpose of a Dutch oven & long covered baker is to emulate a baker's oven by trapping the moisture from the dough in a hot, enclosed, environment. This is an excellent method for making artisan quality bread. Dutch ovens & long covered bakers come in a variety of sizes, shapes and types.

Dutch Ovens: There are three basic sizes... small (2-1/2 to 3 qt), medium (3-1/2 to 4 qt) and large (4-1/2 qt and larger). You can use any size. The key is... the sides of the Dutch oven will shape the loaf. If you use a large Dutch oven the dough will spread giving you a wide low profile loaf. If you use a small Dutch oven the sides will force the dough to rise upward which will give you a tall plump loaf.

Dutch ovens are typically cast iron, but they can be ceramic or pottery. And it should be noted... if you don't have a Dutch oven, you can use any oven proof dish (*CorningWare*, etc.). Ones with heavy lids are better because they will do a better job holding heat and moisture like a Dutch oven.

Long Covered Bakers: Long covered bakers are typically 13-1/2" x 4-1/2". The most popular is the *Sassafras* superstone oblong covered baker. It will give you a very nice long loaf.

Bottom-line: Dutch ovens & long covered bakers do an excellent job of baking the crumb and developing the crust. When I want a round loaf (boule) I use a Dutch oven. When I want a long loaf I use a long covered baker.

No-Knead Bread Recipes using Dutch Oven & Long Covered Baker

Generally speaking, cast iron Dutch ovens are preheated while ceramic Dutch ovens and long covered bakers start at room temperature (like bread pans). Here are three recipes demonstrating the three techniques. And remember, you can use any recipe with these baking techniques.

Country White Bread (preheated cast iron Dutch oven)

This is the basic technique for making an artisan boule (round loaf). I used the traditional method for this loaf, but you can use the "Turbo" method if you wish.

Option:

"Turbo" method... if you wish to reduce the proofing time from 8 hours to 1-1/2 hours... increase yeast from 1/4 to 1-1/4 tsp and proof in a warm draft free environment (78 to 85 degrees F).

Large Loaf... if you wish to increase the size of your loaf for whatever reason... add 2 oz more water, add 1/2 cup more flour (all other ingredients remain the same), and increase baking time by 5 minutes.

Country White Bread

Pour water into a 3 to 4 qt glass mixing bowl.

    <u>14 oz cool Water</u>

Add salt and yeast... give a quick stir to combine.

    <u>1-1/2 tsp Salt</u>
    <u>1/4 tsp Dry Yeast (Instant or Active Dry Yeast)</u>

Add flour... stir until dough forms a shaggy ball, scrape dry flour from side of bowl, then tumble dough to combine moist flour with dry flour.

    <u>3-1/2 cups Bread Flour</u>

Cover bowl with plastic wrap, place on counter, and proof for 8 to 24 hours.

8 to 24 hours later (preheated cast Iron Dutch oven)

When dough has risen and developed its gluten structure... spray an 8" proofing skillet with no-stick cooking spray and set aside.

"Degas, pull and stretch"... stick handle end of a plastic spoon in the dough and stir (dough will form a sticky ball). Then, scrape side of bowl to get remainder of the dough into the sticky dough ball.

Roll dough out of bowl into proofing skillet.

Place proofing skillet in a warm draft-free location, cover with a lint-free towel, and proof for 30 minutes.

Before dough is fully proofed...

Move oven rack to the lower third of the oven, place Dutch oven in oven, and pre-heat to 450 degrees F.

30 minutes later

When the dough has proofed and oven has come to temperature... remove baking vessel from oven, transfer dough from proofing skillet to baking vessel, shake to center, and bake for 30 minutes with the top on and 3 to 15 minutes with the top off depending on how rustic (hard) you like your crust.

33 to 45 minutes later

Remove Dutch oven from oven, gently turn loaf out on work surface and place on cooling rack.

Harvest Grain Country White Bread (ceramic Dutch oven)

This Harvest Grain Country White Bread has a more robust and complex flavor than the multigrain country white. I experimented with and tested a number of my own multigrain mixtures before I discovered *King Arthur's* Harvest Grains Blend and—as they state on their website—the whole oat berries, millet, rye flakes and wheat flakes enhance texture while the flax, poppy, sesame, and sunflower seeds add crunch and great, nutty flavor. Wow, the flavor is great… and it's a lot easier and more practical to purchase a blend of seeds. I used the "Turbo" method for this loaf, but you can use the traditional method if you wish.

Option:

Traditional method… if you wish to use the traditional method… decrease yeast from 1-1/4 tsp to 1/4 tsp and proof 8 to 24 hours.

Large Loaf… if you wish to increase the size of your loaf for whatever reason… add 2 oz more water, add 1/2 cup more flour (all other ingredients remain the same), and increase baking time by 5 minutes.

Harvest Grain Country White Bread

Pour warm water in a 3 to 4 qt warm glass mixing bowl (use a warm bowl... you don't want a cold bowl to take the heat out of the warm water).

<u>16 oz warm Water</u>

Add salt, yeast, grains and olive oil... give a quick stir to combine.

<u>1-1/2 tsp Salt</u>
<u>1-1/4 tsp Dry Yeast (Instant or Active Dry Yeast)</u>
<u>1/2 cup King Arthur Harvest Grains Blend</u>
<u>1 Tbsp extra-virgin Olive Oil</u>

Add flour... stir until dough forms a shaggy ball, scrape dry flour from side of bowl, then tumble dough to combine moist flour with dry flour.

<u>3-1/2 cups Bread Flour</u>

Cover bowl with plastic wrap, place in a warm draft-free location, and proof for 1-1/2 hours.

1-1/2 hours later (ceramic Dutch oven | garnish)

When dough has risen and developed its gluten structure... spray ceramic Dutch oven with no-stick spray and set aside.

"Degas, pull and stretch"... stick handle end of a plastic spoon in the dough and stir (dough will form a sticky ball). Then, scrape side of bowl to get remainder of the dough into the sticky dough ball.

Garnish... sprinkle dough ball and side of bowl with grains, and roll-to-coat (roll dough ball in grains to coat).

<u>2 Tbsp King Arthur Harvest Grains Blend</u>

Roll dough out of bowl into ceramic Dutch oven.

Cover with lid, place in a warm draft-free location, and proof for 30 minutes.

Before dough is fully proofed...

Move oven rack to lower third of the oven and pre-heat to 400 degrees F.

30 minutes later

When the dough has proofed and oven has come to temperature... place Dutch oven in oven and bake for 40 minutes with the top on and 3 to 15 minutes with the top off depending on how rustic (hard) you like your crust.

43 to 55 minutes later

Remove Dutch oven from oven, gently turn loaf out on work surface and place on cooling rack.

Italian Sesame Seed Bread (long covered baker)

Italian sesame seed bread is the ideal recipe for a long covered baker. I used the "Turbo" method for this loaf, but you can use the traditional method if you wish.

Option:

Traditional method... if you wish to use the traditional method... decrease yeast from 1-1/4 tsp to 1/4 tsp and proof 8 to 24 hours.

Large Loaf... if you wish to increase the size of your loaf for whatever reason... add 2 oz more water, add 1/2 cup more flour (all other ingredients remain the same), and increase baking time by 5 minutes.

Supporting video: No-Knead Italian Sesame Seed Bread... baked 4 ways (super easy... no machines)

Italian Sesame Seed Bread

Pour warm water in a 3 to 4 qt warm glass mixing bowl (use a warm bowl... you don't want a cold bowl to take the heat out of the warm water).

    14 oz warm Water

Add salt, yeast, seeds and olive oil... give a quick stir to combine.

    1-1/2 tsp Salt
    1-1/4 tsp Dry Yeast (Instant or Active Dry Yeast)
    1 Tbsp Sesame Seeds
    1 Tbsp extra-virgin Olive Oil

Add flour... stir until dough forms a shaggy ball, scrape dry flour from side of bowl, then tumble dough to combine moist flour with dry flour.

    3-1/2 cups Bread Flour

Cover bowl with plastic wrap, place in a warm draft-free location, and proof for 1-1/2 hours.

1-1/2 hours later (long covered baker | garnish, dust & shape)

When dough has risen and developed its gluten structure... spray baker with no-stick spray and set aside.

"Degas, pull and stretch"... stick handle end of a plastic spoon in the dough and stir (dough will form a sticky ball). Then, scrape side of bowl to get remainder of the dough into the sticky dough ball.

Garnish... sprinkle dough ball and side of bowl with sesame seeds, and roll-to-coat (roll dough ball in seeds to coat).

    2 Tbsp Sesame Seeds

"Roll-to-coat"... sprinkle dough ball and side of bowl with flour and roll-to-coat (dusting dough ball with flour will make it easier to handle and shape the dough for the baker).

    2 Tbsp Bread Flour

Dust work surface with flour, roll dough (and excess flour) out of bowl onto work surface, roll dough on work surface in flour to shape, and place in baker. Cover with lid, place in a warm draft-free location, and proof for 30 minutes.

Before dough is fully proofed...

Move oven rack to lower third of the oven and pre-heat to 400 degrees F.

30 minutes later

When the dough has proofed and oven has come to temperature... place covered baker in oven and bake for 40 minutes with the top on and 3 to 15 minutes with the top off depending on how rustic (hard) you like your crust.

43 to 55 minutes later

Remove covered baker from oven, gently turn loaf out on work surface and place on cooling rack.

Guide to "Poor Man's Dutch Oven" (PMDO)

Simply stated, a "poor man's Dutch oven" (PMDO) is a bread pan covered by another bread pan. The purpose of the bottom bread pan is to shape the loaf into sandwich bread and the purpose of the cover (top bread pan) is to trap the moisture from the dough in a hot, enclosed, environment. The technique emulates a Dutch oven while giving me the desired shape (sandwich bread).

The concept of using a "poor man's Dutch oven" to bake sandwich bread is a new technique, thus I felt it was important to test the options. While testing bread pans I didn't learn anything earth-shaking, but I did learn some good general rules.

Sizes: There are four basic sizes... small (8" x 4") for raisin bread, medium (8-1/2" x 4-1/2") and large (9" x 5") for standard loaves, and long (12" x 4-1/2") for long and half loaves.

The four PMDOs in the picture from left to right are...
- Good Cook premium nonstick loaf pan (8" x 4" x 2-1/4") (Liquid capacity: 42 oz)... excellent for raisin bread and other small (3 cups flour) loaves.
- OXO Good Gripe Non-Stick Pro 1 lb Loaf Pan (8-1/2" x 4-1/2" x 2-4/5") (Liquid capacity: 52 oz)... my personnel favorite.
- Good Cook premium nonstick loaf pan (9" x 5" x 2-1/4") (Liquid capacity: 64 oz)... excellent and inexpensive.
- Wilton long loaf pan (12" x 4-1/2" x 3-1/8") (Liquid capacity: 76 oz)... ideal for long and half loaves (get 4 if you wish to make half loaves).

Liquid capacity is import, because some bread pans are not properly marked.

Shape: You can use either a 9" x 5" or 8-1/2" x 4-1/2" bread pan for a 1 pound loaf (3-1/2 cups flour) but the shape of the loaf will be a little different. The 9" x

5" bread pan will give you a little wider loaf and the 8-1/2" x 4-1/2" bread pan will give you a little taller loaf.

I like pans with flat rims and thin handles. Flat rims… fit together better (snug) and the unit is more stable. Thin handles… allows me to use binder clips.

A snug fit between the pans is important, but it doesn't have to be air tight.

Sometimes little things make a difference. After washing the bread pans I found I liked rounded corners… it's easier to clean the corners.

Fasteners: You really don't need to fasten the top pan to the bottom, but it's more secure and stable. My favorite fastener is the standard binder clip which is available in the office supply section of many stores. I use both medium and large binder clips depending on the shape of the bread pan's handles.

Type: Metal pans were the clear winner. They heat faster and did an excellent job baking the crumb and developing the crust.

Loaf pans made of glass and cast iron did not fare as well. The internal temperature was 200+ degrees F (just like the others), but the crust did not develop as well and the top had a tendency to sag.

YouTube videos in support of recipes: World's Easiest No-Knead Sandwich Bread using a Poor Man's Dutch Oven demonstrates traditional method and How to Bake No-Knead Bread in a Poor Man's Dutch Oven (no mixer… no bread machine) demonstrates "Turbo" method.

No-Knead Bread Recipes using a PMDO

Country White Sandwich Bread (Basic PMDO recipe & technique)
Country white is the most popular bread. It's simple... it's basic. And, if you're making your first PMDO loaf... this is the place to start. I used two *OXO* Good Gripe Non-Stick Pro 1 LB Loaf Pans (8-1/2" x 4-1/2") for my PMDO.

Picture: For lunch I made an egg salad sandwich... a little lettuce and my special egg salad between a couple slices of fresh-from-the-oven classic white bread. To make my special egg salad I use... 12 hard boiled eggs (sliced with a egg slicer and cut down the middle), 4 heaping tbsp mayo, 1 heaping tbsp yellow mustard, 1 heaping tbsp sweet pickle relish and 1 teaspoon salt.

Option:
"Turbo" method... if you wish to reduce the proofing time from 8 hours to 1-1/2 hours... increase yeast from 1/4 to 1-1/4 tsp and proof in a warm draft free environment (78 to 85 degrees F).

Large Loaf... if you wish to increase the size of your loaf for whatever reason... add 2 oz more water, add 1/2 cup more flour (all other ingredients remain the same), and increase baking time by 5 minutes.

Country White Sandwich Bread

Pour water into a 3 to 4 qt glass mixing bowl.
>14 oz cool Water

Add salt and yeast... give a quick stir to combine.
>1-1/2 tsp Salt
>1/4 tsp Dry Yeast (Instant or Active Dry Yeast)

Add flour... stir until dough forms a shaggy ball, scrape dry flour from side of bowl, then tumble dough to combine moist flour with dry flour.
>3-1/2 cups Bread Flour

Cover with plastic wrap and place in a warm draft-free location to proof for 8 to 24 hours.

8 to 24 hours later (PMDO)

When dough has risen and developed its gluten structure... spray bottom bread pan (8-1/2" x 4-1/2" or 9" x 5") with no-stick cooking spray and set aside.
"Degas, pull and stretch"... stick handle end of a plastic spoon in the dough and stir (dough will form a sticky ball). Then, scrape side of bowl to get remainder of the dough into the sticky dough ball.
Roll dough out of bowl into bread pan.
Cover bottom pan with top pan, secure with binder clips, and place PMDO in a warm draft-free location to proof for 30 minutes.

Before dough is fully proofed...

Move rack to lower third of oven and pre-heat to 400 degrees F.

30 minutes later

When the dough has proofed and oven has come to temperature... place PMDO in oven and bake for 40 minutes with the top on.

40 minutes later

Remove PMDO from oven, remove top, place back in oven, and bake for an additional 3 to 15 minutes to finish the crust.

3 to 15 minutes later

Remove PMDO from oven, gently turn loaf out on work surface and place on cooling rack.

Honey Oatmeal Bread (PMDO... standard bread pans)

Fresh-from-the-oven bread with the wholesome goodness of oats and the sweetness of honey... what's not to like? This loaf is as delicious to eat as it is pleasing to the eye. I used two *OXO* Good Gripe Non-Stick Pro 1 LB Loaf Pans (8-1/2" x 4-1/2") for my PMDO.

Picture: For lunch I made a country fried steak sandwich... I spread mayo on two slices fresh-from-the-oven honey oatmeal bread and added 1 precook country fried steak, lettuce and tomato. Simple... surprisingly delicious.

Option:

"Turbo" method... if you wish to reduce the proofing time from 8 hours to 1-1/2 hours... increase yeast from 1/4 to 1-1/4 tsp and proof in a warm draft free environment (78 to 85 degrees F).

Large Loaf... if you wish to increase the size of your loaf for whatever reason... add 2 oz more water, add 1/2 cup more flour (all other ingredients remain the same), and increase baking time by 5 minutes.

Supporting video: No-Knead Honey Oatmeal... (super easy... no mixer... no bread machine) | Original video: No-Knead Honey Oatmeal Bread (Easy... No Mixer... No Yeast Proofing)

Honey Oatmeal Bread

Pour water into a 3 to 4 qt glass mixing bowl.
>16 oz cool Water

Add salt, yeast and honey... give a quick stir to combine.
>1-1/2 tsp Salt
>1/4 tsp Dry Yeast (Instant or Active Dry Yeast)
>1 Tbsp Honey

Add flour... then oats (if oats are added before flour they will absorb the water and it will be harder to combine)... stir until dough forms a shaggy ball, scrape dry flour from side of bowl, then tumble dough to combine moist flour with dry flour.
>3-1/2 cups Bread Flour
>1 cup Old Fashioned *Quaker* Oats

Cover with plastic wrap and place in a warm draft-free location to proof for 8 to 24 hours.

8 to 24 hours later (PMDO - garnish)

When dough has risen and developed its gluten structure... spray bottom bread pan (8-1/2" x 4-1/2" or 9" x 5") with no-stick cooking spray and set aside.

"Degas, pull and stretch"... stick handle end of a plastic spoon in the dough and stir (dough will form a sticky ball). Then, scrape side of bowl to get remainder of the dough into the sticky dough ball.

Garnish... sprinkle dough ball and side of bowl with oats, and roll-to-coat (roll dough ball in oats to coat).
>1/4 cup Old Fashioned *Quaker* Oats

Roll dough out of bowl into bread pan.

Cover bottom pan with top pan, secure with binder clips, and place PMDO in a warm draft-free location to proof for 30 minutes.

Before dough is fully proofed...

Move rack to lower third of oven and pre-heat to 400 degrees F.

30 minutes later

When the dough has proofed and oven has come to temperature... place PMDO in oven and bake for 40 minutes with the top on.

40 minutes later

Remove PMDO from oven, remove top, place back in oven, and bake for an additional 3 to 15 minutes to finish the crust.

3 to 15 minutes later

Remove PMDO from oven, gently turn loaf out on work surface and place on cooling rack.

Honey Whole Wheat Bread (PMDO... standard bread pans)
This whole wheat recipe balances the nutrition and nutty taste of whole wheat with the crumb of a Country White in a hearty, moist loaf with a touch of honey for sweetness. I used two *OXO* Good Gripe Non-Stick Pro 1 LB Loaf Pans (8-1/2" x 4-1/2") for my PMDO.

Picture: For lunch I made a deli-fresh turkey, ham and cheese sandwich. I spread mayo on two slices fresh-from-the-oven honey whole wheat bread, added several slices of turkey and ham, then topped it with lettuce and tomato, and I put provolone cheese on one and Swiss on the other.

Option:
"Turbo" method... if you wish to reduce the proofing time from 8 hours to 1-1/2 hours... increase yeast from 1/4 to 1-1/4 tsp and proof in a warm draft free environment (78 to 85 degrees F).

Large Loaf... if you wish to increase the size of your loaf for whatever reason... add 2 oz more water, add 1/2 cup more flour (all other ingredients remain the same), and increase baking time by 5 minutes.

Honey Whole Wheat Bread

Pour water into a 3 to 4 qt glass mixing bowl.

> 16 oz cool Water

Add salt, yeast, olive oil and honey... give a quick stir to combine.

> 1-1/2 tsp Salt
> 1/4 tsp Dry Yeast (Instant or Active Dry Yeast)
> 1 Tbsp extra-virgin Olive Oil
> 1 Tbsp Honey

Add flour... stir until dough forms a shaggy ball, scrape dry flour from side of bowl, then tumble dough to combine moist flour with dry flour.

> 2 cups Bread Flour
> 1-1/2 cups Whole Wheat Flour

Cover with plastic wrap and place in a warm draft-free location to proof for 8 to 24 hours.

8 to 24 hours later (PMDO)

When dough has risen and developed its gluten structure... spray bottom bread pan (8-1/2" x 4-1/2" or 9" x 5") with no-stick cooking spray and set aside.

"Degas, pull and stretch"... stick handle end of a plastic spoon in the dough and stir (dough will form a sticky ball). Then, scrape side of bowl to get remainder of the dough into the sticky dough ball.

Roll dough out of bowl into bread pan.

Cover bottom pan with top pan, secure with binder clips, and place PMDO in a warm draft-free location to proof for 30 minutes.

Before dough is fully proofed...

Move rack to lower third of oven and pre-heat to 400 degrees F.

30 minutes later

When the dough has proofed and oven has come to temperature... place PMDO in oven and bake for 40 minutes with the top on.

40 minutes later

Remove PMDO from oven, remove top, place back in oven, and bake for an additional 3 to 15 minutes to finish the crust.

3 to 15 minutes later

Remove PMDO from oven, gently turn loaf out on work surface and place on cooling rack.

Garlic Bread (PMDO... long bread pans)

All of us like garlic cheese bread... I like to lightly infuse the garlic into the loaf. It gives the loaf a nice full flavor and it's easier than adding garlic after the fact. I used two *Wilton* 12" x 4-1/2" long bread pans for my PMDO.

Note: This recipe calls for 1 to 2 heaping tsp minced garlic (jar). I generally use 1, but it's a personal taste issue. Try both and see which you like.

Picture: As an appetizer for dinner I served garlic cheese bread. Because the garlic is already infused in the bread, all I needed to do was... toast two slices, spread on a little butter, add a little cheese, a sprinkle of salt, and broil them in the toaster oven to melt the cheese.

Options:
Standard vs. long bread pan... use the same ingredients and increase baking time with the top on by 5 minutes.
"Turbo" method... if you wish to reduce the proofing time from 8 hours to 1-1/2 hours... increase yeast from 1/4 to 1-1/4 tsp and proof in a warm draft free environment (78 to 85 degrees F).

Large Loaf... if you wish to increase the size of your loaf for whatever reason... add 2 oz more water, add 1/2 cup more flour (all other ingredients remain the same), and increase baking time by 5 minutes.

Supporting video: No-Knead Garlic Bread... super easy... foolproof... no machines

Garlic Bread

Pour water into a 3 to 4 qt glass mixing bowl.
>14 oz cool Water

Add salt, yeast, garlic and olive oil... give a quick stir to combine.
>1-1/2 tsp Salt
>1/4 tsp Dry Yeast (Instant or Active Dry Yeast)
>1 to 2 heaping tsp Minced Garlic (jar)
>1 Tbsp extra-virgin Olive Oil

Add flour... stir until dough forms a shaggy ball, scrape dry flour from side of bowl, then tumble dough to combine moist flour with dry flour.
>3-1/2 cups Bread Flour

Cover with plastic wrap and place in a warm draft-free location to proof for 8 to 24 hours.

8 to 24 hours later (long PMDO – dust & shape)

When dough has risen and developed its gluten structure... spray bottom bread pan (8-1/2" x 4-1/2" or 9" x 5") with no-stick cooking spray and set aside.

"Degas, pull and stretch"... stick handle end of a plastic spoon in the dough and stir (dough will form a sticky ball). Then, scrape side of bowl to get remainder of the dough into the sticky dough ball.

"Roll-to-coat"... sprinkle dough ball and side of bowl with flour and roll-to-coat (dusting dough ball with flour will make it easier to handle and shape the dough for the baker).
>2 Tbsp Bread Flour

Dust work surface with flour, roll dough (and excess flour) out of bowl onto work surface, roll dough on work surface in flour to shape, and place in long PMDO.

Cover bottom pan with top pan, secure with binder clips, and place PMDO in a warm draft-free location to proof for 30 minutes.

Before dough is fully proofed...

Move rack to lower third of oven and pre-heat to 400 degrees F.

30 minutes later

When the dough has proofed and oven has come to temperature... place PMDO in oven and bake for 35 minutes with the top on.

35 minutes later

Remove PMDO from oven, remove top, place back in oven, and bake for an additional 3 to 15 minutes to finish the crust.

3 to 15 minutes later

Remove PMDO from oven, gently turn loaf out on work surface and place on cooling rack.

No-Knead Bread (PMDO... baked in a toaster oven)

No oven... no problem... you can bake no-knead bread in a toaster oven. This technique is ideal for those with limited kitchens and those of you who don't want to turn the oven on because it heats the house in the summer. This technique is effective with a PMDO (8-1/2" x 4-1/2" and 9" x 5") and *Sassafras* superstone oblong covered baker (13-1/2" x 4-1/2").

Background: I made several attempts to bake bread in a toaster oven with poor results until I developed the PMDO. The problem was... the heating element was too close to the top of the loaf. I now bake 80% of my bread using a PMDO in the toaster oven. My wife is thrilled because I don't heat the kitchen in the summer.

YouTube videos in support of recipe: "How to Bake No-Knead Bread in a Toaster Oven (no mixer... no bread machine... "hands-free" technique)"

Option:
Traditional method... if you wish to use the traditional method... decrease yeast from 1-1/4 tsp to 1/4 tsp and proof 8 to 24 hours.

Large Loaf... if you wish to increase the size of your loaf for whatever reason... add 2 oz more water, add 1/2 cup more flour (all other ingredients remain the same), and increase baking time by 5 minutes.

Country White Bread

Pour warm water in a 3 to 4 qt warm glass mixing bowl (use a warm bowl... you don't want a cold bowl to take the heat out of the warm water).

> 14 oz warm Water

Add salt and yeast... give a quick stir to combine.

> 1-1/2 tsp Salt
> 1-1/4 tsp Dry Yeast (Instant or Active Dry Yeast)

Add flour... stir until dough forms a shaggy ball, scrape dry flour from side of bowl, then tumble dough to combine moist flour with dry flour.

> 3-1/2 cups Bread Flour

Cover bowl with plastic wrap, place bowl under a desk lamp, lower lamp so that it's close to the bowl, turn lamp on, and proof for 1-1/2 hours (see note below).

1-1/2 hours later (PMDO in a toaster oven)

When dough has risen and developed its gluten structure... spray bottom bread pan (8-1/2" x 4-1/2" or 9" x 5") with no-stick cooking spray and set aside.
"Degas, pull and stretch"... stick handle end of a plastic spoon in the dough and stir (dough will form a sticky ball). Then, scrape side of bowl to get remainder of the dough into the sticky dough ball.
Roll dough out of bowl into bread pan.
Cover bottom pan with top pan, secure with binder clips, and place PMDO in a warm draft-free location to proof for 30 minutes.

30 minutes later

Place PMDO in toaster oven, set oven to 400 degrees F, and bake for 45 minutes.

45 minutes later

Remove PMDO from oven, gently turn loaf out on work surface and place on cooling rack.

Note:

The ideal proofing temperature is 78 to 85 degrees F, but most of our homes are 68 to 73 degrees. So... to create a favorable proofing environment I place the bowl under my desk lamp where the plastic wrap on the bowl traps the heat and raise the temperature inside the bowl to a little over 80 degrees (solar affect).

Author's Note

No-knead bread has been around for years.
For example, here's a 1739 recipe to make
French bread that was published in
"The Compleat Housewife"
(by Eliza Smith)
which states
"stir it about with your hand,
but by no means knead it".

To make French Bread.

TAKE half a peck of fine flour, put to it six yolks of eggs, and four whites, a little salt, a pint of good ale-yeast, and as much new milk, made a little warm, as will make it a thin light paste; stir it about with your hand, but by no means knead it; then have ready six wooden quart dishes, and fill them with dough; let them stand a quarter of an hour to heave, and then turn them out into the oven; and when they are bak'd, rasp them: the oven must be quick.

To learn more about the history of no-knead bread
go to
http://nokneadbreadcentral.com/.
for the written version or watch
Quick History of No-Knead Bread

Additional Bread Recipes

One simple recipe… four ingredients, no mixer, no kneading, no yeast proofing… just a little tweaking and you can create a variety of artisan breads that you would be proud to serve your family, friends and guests.

I will be using a variety of different baking vessels/methods to make the breads… Dutch oven, long baker, baking stone, baguette pan, parchment paper, silicone pad, and a rimmed baking sheet… and, generally speaking you can take the ingredients from one recipe and use the baking vessel/method from a different recipe. Thus, if you wish to bake the caraway rye bread in a Dutch oven… take the ingredients from the caraway rye bread recipe and use the method and baking times from a recipe using a Dutch oven… baking for 30 minutes with the top on and 3 to 15 minutes with the top off.

There are two methods for making no-knead bread… "Traditional" (proofs for 8 to 24 hours) and "Turbo" (ready to bake in 2-1/2 hours). We'll start with the traditional because it is easier and more popular.

Cheddar Cheese Bread (Dutch oven)

Bread is one of the great comfort foods. Fresh from the oven bread is something special... add cheese and you have a winner. Something your friends and guests will love. This is a remarkably simple recipe that is as delicious as it looks. I used a 3 qt *Lodge* Enameled cast iron Dutch oven to shape this loaf.

Option:

"Turbo" method... if you wish to reduce the proofing time from 8 hours to 1-1/2 hours... increase yeast from 1/4 to 1-1/4 tsp and proof in a warm draft free environment (78 to 85 degrees F).

Large Loaf... if you wish to increase the size of your loaf for whatever reason... add 2 oz more water, add 1/2 cup more flour (all other ingredients remain the same), and increase baking time by 5 minutes.

Supporting video: No-Knead Cheddar Cheese Bread & Rolls (updated)... super easy... no machines

Cheddar Cheese Bread

Pour water into a 3 to 4 qt glass mixing bowl.

    16 oz cool tap Water

Add salt and yeast... give a quick stir to combine.

    1-1/2 tsp Salt

    1/4 tsp Dry Yeast (Instant or Active Dry Yeast)

Add flour... then cheese (if cheese is added before flour it will be harder to combine)... stir until dough forms a shaggy ball, scrape dry flour from side of bowl, then tumble dough to combine moist flour with dry flour.

    3-1/2 cups Bread Flour

    1 cup coarse shredded Cheddar Cheese

Cover bowl with plastic wrap, place on counter, and proof for 8 to 24 hours.

8 to 24 hours later (preheated cast Iron Dutch oven)

When dough has risen and developed its gluten structure... spray an 8" proofing skillet with no-stick cooking spray and set aside.

"Degas, pull and stretch"... stick handle end of a plastic spoon in the dough and stir (dough will form a sticky ball). Then, scrape side of bowl to get remainder of the dough into the sticky dough ball.

Roll dough out of bowl into proofing skillet.

Place proofing skillet in a warm draft-free location, cover with a lint-free towel, and proof for 30 minutes.

Before dough is fully proofed...

Move oven rack to the lower third of the oven, place Dutch oven in oven, and pre-heat to 450 degrees F.

30 minutes later

When the dough has proofed and oven has come to temperature... remove baking vessel from oven, transfer dough from proofing skillet to baking vessel, shake to center, and bake for 30 minutes with the top on and 3 to 15 minutes with the top off depending on how rustic (hard) you like your crust.

33 to 45 minutes later

Remove Dutch oven from oven, gently turn loaf out on work surface and place on cooling rack.

Multigrain Whole Wheat Bread (PMDO)

This is very similar to the Multigrain Country White, except with wheat flour. It's intended to be a simple loaf with broad general appeal. If you haven't made wheat bread before, this is an excellent choice for your first loaf. Simple recipe... simple flavors... universally pleasing taste. I use 2 cups bread flour with 1-1/2 cups whole wheat flour because that's my preference, but you can use all whole wheat flour if you wish.

Picture: Picture is from the updated video (link below) in which I made two loaves. I used two OXO 4-1/2" x 8-1/2" bread pans for the PMDO and a Sassafras superstone long covered baker for the long loaf.

Option:

"Turbo" method... if you wish to reduce the proofing time from 8 hours to 1-1/2 hours... increase yeast from 1/4 to 1-1/4 tsp and proof in a warm draft free environment (78 to 85 degrees F).

Large Loaf... if you wish to increase the size of your loaf for whatever reason... add 2 oz more water, add 1/2 cup more flour (all other ingredients remain the same), and increase baking time by 5 minutes.

Supporting video: No-Knead Multigrain Whole Wheat Bread... super easy... no machines (updated)

Multigrain Whole Wheat Bread

Pour water into a 3 to 4 qt glass mixing bowl.
>16 oz cool tap Water

Add salt, yeast, seeds, and olive oil... give a quick stir to combine.
>1-1/2 tsp Salt
>1/4 tsp Dry Yeast (Instant or Active Dry Yeast)
>1 Tbsp Sesame Seeds
>1 Tbsp Flax Seeds
>1 Tbsp extra-virgin Olive Oil

Add flour... then oats (if oats are added before flour they will absorb the water and it will be harder to combine)... stir until dough forms a shaggy ball, scrape dry flour from side of bowl, then tumble dough to combine moist flour with dry flour.
>2 cups Bread Flour
>1-1/2 cup Whole Wheat Flour
>1/2 cup Old Fashioned *Quaker* Oats

Cover bowl with plastic wrap, place on counter, and proof for 8 to 24 hours.

8 to 24 hours later (PMDO - garnish)

When dough has risen and developed its gluten structure... spray bottom bread pan (8-1/2" x 4-1/2" or 9" x 5") with no-stick cooking spray and set aside.

"Degas, pull and stretch"... stick handle end of a plastic spoon in the dough and stir (dough will form a sticky ball). Then, scrape side of bowl to get remainder of the dough into the sticky dough ball.

Garnish... sprinkle dough ball and side of bowl with oats, and roll-to-coat (roll dough ball in oats to coat).
>1/4 cup Old Fashioned *Quaker* Oats

Roll dough out of bowl into bread pan.

Cover bottom pan with top pan, secure with binder clips, and place PMDO in a warm draft-free location to proof for 30 minutes.

Before dough is fully proofed...

Move rack to lower third of oven and pre-heat to 400 degrees F.

30 minutes later

When the dough has proofed and oven has come to temperature... place PMDO in oven and bake for 40 minutes with the top on.

40 minutes later

Remove PMDO from oven, remove top, place back in oven, and bake for an additional 3 to 15 minutes to finish the crust.

3 to 15 minutes later

Remove PMDO from oven, gently turn loaf out on work surface and place on cooling rack.

Harvest Grains Honey Whole Wheat Bread (Dutch oven)
This Harvest Grains Honey Whole Wheat Bread has a more robust and complex flavor than the multigrain country white and wheat breads. I experimented with and tested a number of my own multigrain mixtures before I discovered King Arthur's Harvest Grains Blend. And—as they state on their website—the whole oat berries, millet, rye flakes and wheat flakes enhance texture while the flax, poppy, sesame, and sunflower seeds add crunch and great, nutty flavor. Wow, the flavor is great... and it's a lot easier and more practical to purchase a blend of seeds. I used our *Lodge* 3 qt cast iron Dutch oven to shape this loaf.

Option:
"Turbo" method... if you wish to reduce the proofing time from 8 hours to 1-1/2 hours... increase yeast from 1/4 to 1-1/4 tsp and proof in a warm draft free environment (78 to 85 degrees F).

Large Loaf... if you wish to increase the size of your loaf for whatever reason... add 2 oz more water, add 1/2 cup more flour (all other ingredients remain the same), and increase baking time by 5 minutes.

Supporting video: No-Knead Harvest Grains Honey Whole Wheat Bread (updated)... super easy

Harvest Grains Honey Whole Wheat Bread

Pour water into a 3 to 4 qt glass mixing bowl.
>16 oz cool tap Water

Add salt, yeast, grains, olive oil, honey... and give a quick stir to combine.
>1-1/2 tsp Salt
>1/4 tsp Dry Yeast (Instant or Active Dry Yeast)
>1/2 cup King Arthur Harvest Grains Blend
>1 Tbsp extra-virgin Olive Oil
>1 Tbsp Honey

Add flour... stir until dough forms a shaggy ball, scrape dry flour from side of bowl, then tumble dough to combine moist flour with dry flour.
>2 cups Bread Flour
>1-1/2 cup Whole Wheat Flour

Cover bowl with plastic wrap, place on counter, and proof for 8 to 24 hours.

8 to 24 hours later (preheated cast iron Dutch oven | garnish & dust)

When dough has risen and developed its gluten structure... spray an 8" proofing skillet with no-stick cooking spray and set aside.

"Degas, pull and stretch"... stick handle end of a plastic spoon in the dough and stir (dough will form a sticky ball). Then, scrape side of bowl to get remainder of the dough into the sticky dough ball.

Garnish... sprinkle dough ball and side of bowl with grains and roll-to-coat (roll dough ball in grains to coat).
>2 Tbsp King Arthur Harvest Grains Blend

"Roll-to-coat"... sprinkle dough ball and side of bowl with flour and roll-to-coat (roll dough ball in flour to coat).
>2 Tbsp Flour

Roll dough out of bowl into proofing skillet.

Place proofing skillet in a warm draft-free location, cover with a lint-free towel, and proof for 30 minutes.

Before dough is fully proofed...

Move oven rack to the lower third of the oven, place Dutch oven in oven, and pre-heat to 450 degrees F.

30 minutes later

When the dough has proofed and oven has come to temperature... remove baking vessel from oven, transfer dough from proofing skillet to baking vessel, shake to center, and bake for 30 minutes with the top on and 3 to 15 minutes with the top off depending on how rustic (hard) you like your crust.

33 to 45 minutes later

Remove Dutch oven from oven, gently turn loaf out on work surface and place on cooling rack.

Sunflower Seed & Honey Whole Wheat (Dutch oven)
The sweetness of honey with sunflower seeds... a beautiful loaf that is sure to please. I used a 3 qt *Lodge* Enameled cast iron Dutch oven to shape this loaf.

Option:
"Turbo" method... if you wish to reduce the proofing time from 8 hours to 1-1/2 hours... increase yeast from 1/4 to 1-1/4 tsp and proof in a warm draft free environment (78 to 85 degrees F).

Large Loaf... if you wish to increase the size of your loaf for whatever reason... add 2 oz more water, add 1/2 cup more flour (all other ingredients remain the same), and increase baking time by 5 minutes.

Supporting video: No-Knead Sunflower Seed Honey Whole Wheat Bread (updated)... super easy... no machines

Sunflower Seed & Honey Whole Wheat Bread

Pour water into a 3 to 4 qt glass mixing bowl.
>14 oz cool tap Water

Add salt, yeast, honey, seeds and oil... give a quick stir to combine.
>1-1/2 tsp Salt
>1/4 tsp Dry Yeast (Instant or Active Dry Yeast)
>1 Tbsp Vegetable Oil
>2 Tbsp Honey
>1/2 cup Sunflower Seeds

Add flour... stir until dough forms a shaggy ball, scrape dry flour from side of bowl, then tumble dough to combine moist flour with dry flour.
>2 cups Bread Flour
>1-1/2 cup Whole Wheat Flour

Cover bowl with plastic wrap, place on counter, and proof for 8 to 24 hours.

8 to 24 hours later (preheated cast iron Dutch oven | garnish & baste)

When dough has risen and developed its gluten structure... spray an 8" proofing skillet with no-stick cooking spray and set aside.

"Degas, pull and stretch"... stick handle end of a plastic spoon in the dough and stir (dough will form a sticky ball). Then, scrape side of bowl to get remainder of the dough into the sticky dough ball.

Garnish... sprinkle dough ball and side of bowl with seeds and roll-to-coat (roll dough ball in grains to coat).
>2 Tbsp Sunflower Seeds

Baste... place 1 egg yolk in a small mixing bowl, add water, and whip to combine. Then pour egg wash into proofing skillet, swirl to coat skillet and discard excess.
>1 Egg Yolk
>Splash of Water

Roll dough out of bowl into proofing skillet.

Place proofing skillet in a warm draft-free location, cover with a lint-free towel, and proof for 30 minutes.

Before dough is fully proofed...

Move oven rack to the lower third of the oven, place Dutch oven in oven, and pre-heat to 450 degrees F.

30 minutes later

When the dough has proofed and oven has come to temperature... remove baking vessel from oven, transfer dough from proofing skillet to baking vessel (invert so that garnished and basted bottom is on top), shake to center, and bake for 30 minutes with the top on and 3 to 15 minutes with the top off depending on how rustic (hard) you like your crust.

33 to 45 minutes later

Remove Dutch oven from oven, gently turn loaf out on work surface and place on cooling rack.

Mediterranean Olive Bread (long covered baker | half loaves)
If a restaurant served you this loaf as their signature bread... you'd be talking about it for years and you'd be surprised how easy it is to make. I used our *Sassafras* superstone oblong covered bakers to shape these loaves.

Options:
"Turbo" method... if you wish to reduce the proofing time from 8 hours to 1-1/2 hours... increase yeast from 1/4 to 1-1/4 tsp and proof in a warm draft free environment (78 to 85 degrees F).

Large Loaf... if you wish to increase the size of your loaf for whatever reason... add 2 oz more water, add 1/2 cup more flour (all other ingredients remain the same), and increase baking time by 5 minutes.

Supporting video: No-Knead Mediterranean Olive Bread... super easy... 5 Star restaurant quality (updated) | Original video: No-Knead Mediterranean Olive Bread (Easy... No Mixer... No Yeast Proofing)

Mediterranean Olive Bread
Prep: Open black olive can, drain liquid, and place olives in a 1 qt bowl.
    2-1/4 oz (1 can) sliced Black Olives
Use the black olive can (it's about 1/2 cup) to measure green olives and kalamata olives... then slice olives in half and add to bowl.
    1/2 cup stuffed Green Olives
    1/2 cup pitted Kalamata Olives

Zest lemon over bowl and set bowl aside.
>	Zest of 1 Lemon

Make dough: Pour water into a 3 to 4 qt glass mixing bowl.
>	16 oz cool tap Water

Add salt, yeast, thyme, and olive oil... and give a quick stir to combine.
>	1-1/2 tsp Salt
>	1/4 tsp Dry Yeast (Instant or Active Dry Yeast)
>	1 heaping tsp dried Thyme
>	1 Tbsp extra-virgin Olive Oil

Add flour to bowl... then add olive mixture on top of flour. Stir until dough/olive mixture forms a shaggy ball, scrape dry flour from side of bowl, then tumble dough to combine moist flour with dry flour.
>	4 cups Bread Flour

Cover bowl with plastic wrap, place on counter, and proof for 8 to 24 hours.

8 to 24 hours later (long covered baker | half loaves)

When dough has risen and developed its gluten structure... set two 12" x 12" sheets of parchment paper off to the side.

"Degas, pull and stretch"... stick handle end of a plastic spoon in the dough and stir (dough will form a sticky ball). Then, scrape side of bowl to get remainder of the dough into the sticky dough ball.

"Roll-to-coat"... sprinkle dough ball and side of bowl with flour and roll-to-coat (dusting dough ball with flour will make it easier to handle and shape dough).
>	2 Tbsp Bread Flour

Dust work surface with flour, roll dough (and excess flour) out of bowl onto work surface.

Divide dough into 2 portions.

Then (one portion at a time) roll dough on work surface (dusting with flour as needed), form a round ball then roll it on the work surface to lengthen, and place on parchment paper.

>	(a) If you have 2 long covered bakers... use parchment paper as a sling to lift dough up, and place in bakers to proof.
>	(b) If you only have one covered baker... place one in baker to proof and cover 2nd loaf with a lint-free towel to proof until first loaf is baked.

Proof for 30 to 60 minutes.

Before dough is fully proofed...

Move rack to lower third of oven and pre-heat oven to 400 degrees F.

30 minutes later

When the dough has proofed and oven has come to temperature... place bakers in oven and bake for 40 minutes with the top on and 5 to 10 minutes with the top off.

45 to 55 minutes later

Gently turn loaf out on work surface and place on cooling rack.

Skillet Bread (skillet)

Simple recipe… simple technique… great results, and I garnished the loaf with sesame seed. It's really very simple. I didn't even have to touch the dough.

I used a *Lodge* cast iron 10-1/2" skillet to shape this loaf, but you can use any 8" to 10-1/2" oven safe skillet (make sure the handle is oven safe). A smaller 8" skillet will constrain the dough during oven bounce and force the dough to expand upwards and give you a tall plump boule, while a larger 10-1/2" skillet will allow the dough to expand outwards filling the skillet and give you a broad low profile boule.

Option:
Traditional method… if you wish to use the traditional method… decrease yeast from 1-1/4 tsp to 1/4 tsp and proof 8 to 24 hours.

Large Loaf… if you wish to increase the size of your loaf for whatever reason… add 2 oz more water, add 1/2 cup more flour (all other ingredients remain the same), and increase baking time by 5 minutes.

Supporting video (using traditional method): How to Bake No-Knead Bread in a Skillet (updated)… super easy… no machines | Original video: How to Bake No-Knead "Turbo" Bread in a Skillet (ready to bake in 2-1/2 hours) |

Skillet Bread

Pour warm water in a 3 to 4 qt warm glass mixing bowl (use a warm bowl... you don't want a cold bowl to take the heat out of the warm water).

    14 oz warm Water

Add salt and yeast... give a quick stir to combine.

    1-1/2 tsp Salt
    1-1/4 tsp Dry Yeast (Instant or Active Dry Yeast)

Add flour... stir until dough forms a shaggy ball, scrape dry flour from side of bowl, then tumble dough to combine moist flour with dry flour.

    3-1/2 cups Bread Flour

Cover bowl with plastic wrap, place in a warm draft-free location, and proof for 1-1/2 hours.

1-1/2 hours later (skillet | garnish)

When dough has risen and developed its gluten structure... spray skillet with no-stick cooking spray, and set aside.

"Degas, pull and stretch"... stick handle end of a plastic spoon in the dough and stir (dough will form a sticky ball). Then, scrape side of bowl to get remainder of the dough into the sticky dough ball.

Garnish... sprinkle dough ball and side of bowl with sesame seeds and roll-to-coat (roll dough ball in sesame seeds to coat).

    2 Tbsp Sesame Seeds

Roll dough out of bowl into skillet.

Place skillet in a warm draft-free location, cover with a lint-free towel, and proof for 30 minutes.

Before dough is fully proofed...

Move rack to middle of oven and pre-heat to 400 degrees F.

30 minutes later

When the dough has proofed and oven has come to temperature... place skillet in oven and bake for 40 minutes.

40 minutes later

Remove skillet from oven, gently turn loaf out on work surface and place on cooling rack.

Author's Note

Bakers have known for years that
bread benefits from long proofing times.
The no-knead method takes advantage of this principle.
It uses a minimum amount of yeast
and long proofing time to develop flavor.
Meanwhile, the long proofing time
replaces the arduous task of kneading...
Mother Nature does the work for you.

It's smart... it's easy... it's delicious.

Rolls & Buns

Bread is an important part of the meal... it starts the dining experience. Good rolls... good restaurant. Great rolls... great restaurant. Likewise, fresh from the oven rolls & buns can elevate your family's dining experience.

These recipes have a dual purpose... ingredients (recipes) for a variety of rolls and a variety of techniques for shaping the rolls. The important point is... you can use the ingredients from one recipe and the technique for shaping the rolls from another recipe. The options are endless.

Easy Dinner Rolls ("Turbo" method | jumbo muffin pans)
These dinner rolls are simple and basic. If you're making your first batch of rolls this is the place to start… the rolls don't require any shaping. Just "plop" the dough in a jumbo muffin pan and the pan will shape the rolls for you. I used 2 *Wilton* jumbo muffin pans to shape the rolls.

Supporting video: Introduction to No-Knead Turbo Rolls (World's Easiest Dinner Rolls… Ready to Bake in 2-1/2 Hours)

Option:
Traditional method… if you wish to use the traditional method… decrease yeast from 1-1/4 tsp to 1/4 tsp and proof 8 to 24 hours.

Easy Dinner Rolls

Pour warm water in a 3 to 4 qt warm glass mixing bowl (use a warm bowl... you don't want a cold bowl to take the heat out of the warm water).

>14 oz warm Water

Add salt and yeast... give a quick stir to combine.

>1-1/2 tsp Salt
>1-1/4 tsp Dry Yeast (Instant or Active Dry Yeast)

Add flour... stir until dough forms a shaggy ball, scrape dry flour from side of bowl, then tumble dough to combine moist flour with dry flour.

>3-1/2 cups Bread Flour

Cover bowl with plastic wrap, place in a warm draft-free location, and proof for 1-1/2 hours.

1-1/2 hours later (jumbo muffin pans)

When dough has risen and developed its gluten structure... spray 8 cavities in 2 jumbo muffin pans with no-stick cooking spray and set aside.

"Degas, pull and stretch"... stick handle end of a plastic spoon in the dough and stir (dough will form a sticky ball). Then, scrape side of bowl to get remainder of the dough into the sticky dough ball.

"Roll-to-coat"... sprinkle dough ball and side of bowl with flour and roll-to-coat (dusting dough ball with flour will make it easier to handle and shape dough).

>2 Tbsp Bread Flour

Dust work surface with flour, roll dough (and excess flour) out of bowl onto work surface.

Press lightly to flatten... then divide dough into 8 portions (I divide dough in to 4 portions, then divide each portion in half) and place one portion in each cavity (cavity will shape roll).

Place rolls in a warm draft-free location, cover with a lint-free towel, and proof for 30 minutes.

Before dough is fully proofed...

Move rack to middle of oven and pre-heat to 450 degrees F.

30 minutes later

When dough has proofed and oven has come to temperature... place pans in oven and bake for 15 minutes.

15 minutes later

Remove pans from oven and place rolls on a cooling rack.

Pull-Apart Dinner Rolls (silicone baking pad)
One of the beauties of this recipe is that you don't have to handle, shape or move the rolls from the work surface. Use a rolling pin to spread the dough, divide into sections with a pizza cutter and "poof"... you have pull-apart dinner rolls. I used a standard non-stick silicone baking mat (11-5/8" x 16-1/2") for the work surface and baking, but you can also use a cookie sheet. I like to serve them hot from the oven and you'll be very pleased with how the olive oil enhances the crust. They're smart, they're easy, they're delicious.

Note: It is not necessary to spray the silicone baking mat with no stick spray, but you would need to if you baked directly on the cookie sheet.

Option:
"Turbo" method... if you wish to reduce the proofing time from 8 hours to 1-1/2 hours... increase yeast from 1/4 to 1-1/4 tsp and proof in a warm draft free environment (78 to 85 degrees F).

Pull-Apart Dinner Rolls

Pour water into a 3 to 4 qt glass mixing bowl.
>14 oz cool tap Water

Add salt and yeast... give a quick stir to combine.
>1-1/2 tsp Salt
>1/4 tsp Dry Yeast (Instant or Active Dry Yeast)

Add flour... stir until dough forms a shaggy ball, scrape dry flour from side of bowl, then tumble dough to combine moist flour with dry flour.
>3-1/2 cups Bread Flour

Cover bowl with plastic wrap, place on counter, and proof for 8 to 24 hours.

8 to 24 hours later (silicone baking pad)

When dough has risen and developed its gluten structure... place silicone baking mat on a cookie sheet and set aside.

"Degas, pull and stretch"... stick handle end of a plastic spoon in the dough and stir (dough will form a sticky ball). Then, scrape side of bowl to get remainder of the dough into the sticky dough ball.

Baste... drizzle dough and side of bowl with oil... roll dough in oil to coat.
>1 Tbsp Vegetable Oil

Roll dough (and excess oil) out of bowl onto silicone baking mat.

Use a rolling pin (or pizza/pastry roller) to spread dough until it covers 80% of the mat.

Then use a pizza cutter (be careful not to cut through the mat) to divide the dough into sections.

Slide cookie sheet under silicone baking mat, place in a warm draft-free location, cover with a lint-free towel, and proof for 30 to 60 minutes.

Before dough is fully proofed...

Move rack to middle of oven and pre-heat to 450 degrees F.

30 to 60 minutes later

When dough has proofed and oven has come to temperature... slide cookie sheet into oven and bake for 20 minutes.

20 minutes later

Remove from oven and place rolls on a cooling rack.

Garlic-Herb Rolls (mini round cake pans)
If you like olive oil, garlic and herbs you'll love these rolls. They're easy to make and sure to please. You can use 1/2 tsp each dry Marjoram, Thyme, Basil & Oregano or 2 tsp dry Italian Herb Mix if it's more convenient. And... I used 8 *Wilton* mini round cake pans to shape the rolls.

Option:
Traditional method... if you wish to use the traditional method... decrease yeast from 1-1/4 tsp to 1/4 tsp and proof 8 to 24 hours.

Garlic-Herb Rolls
Pour warm water in a 3 to 4 qt warm glass mixing bowl (use a warm bowl... you don't want a cold bowl to take the heat out of the warm water).
    14 oz warm Water
Add salt, yeast, herbs, garlic and olive oil... give a quick stir to combine.
    1-1/2 tsp Salt
    1-1/4 tsp Dry Yeast (Instant or Active Dry Yeast)
    1/2 tsp dry Marjoram
    1/2 tsp dry Thyme
    1/2 tsp dry Basil
    1/2 tsp dry Oregano

    <u>1 to 2 tsp Garlic Paste or minced Garlic</u>
    <u>1 Tbsp extra-virgin Olive Oil</u>

Add flour… then cheese… and stir until dough forms a shaggy ball, scrape dry flour from side of bowl, then tumble dough to combine moist flour with dry flour.

    <u>3-1/2 cups Bread Flour</u>
    <u>1/2 cup shredded Parmesan Cheese</u>

Cover bowl with plastic wrap, place in a warm draft-free location, and proof for 1-1/2 hours.

1-1/2 hours later (mini round cake pan)

When dough has risen and developed its gluten structure… spray 8 mini round cake pans (4" x 1-1/4") with no-stick cooking spray, place in rimmed baking sheet (makes them easier to carry), and set aside.

"Degas, pull and stretch"… stick handle end of a plastic spoon in the dough and stir (dough will form a sticky ball). Then, scrape side of bowl to get remainder of the dough into the sticky dough ball.

"Roll-to-coat"… sprinkle dough ball and side of bowl with flour and roll-to-coat (dusting dough ball with flour will make it easier to handle and shape dough).

    <u>2 Tbsp Bread Flour</u>

Dust work surface with flour, roll dough (and excess flour) out of bowl onto work surface.

Press lightly to flatten… then divide dough into 8 portions (like a pizza) and place one in each pan (pan will shape roll).

Place pans in a warm draft-free location, cover with a lint-free towel, and proof for 30 minutes.

Before dough is fully proofed…

Move rack to middle of oven and pre-heat to 450 degrees F.

30 minutes later

When dough has proofed and oven has come to temperature… slide rimmed baking sheet in oven and bake for 20 minutes.

20 minutes later

Remove from oven, gently turn rolls out on work surface, and place on cooling rack.

Small Sandwich Rolls (mini loaf pans)

Look at the crumb... these rolls will make any sandwich special and the mini loaf pans made them uniform in shape. I used 8 *Chicago Metallic* non-stick mini loaf pans (5-3/4" x 3-1/4" x 2-1/4") to shape these rolls (they are very reasonably priced and come in a three pack).

Option:

<u>Traditional method</u>... if you wish to use the traditional method... decrease yeast from 1-1/4 tsp to 1/4 tsp and proof 8 to 24 hours.

Small Sandwich Rolls

Pour warm water in a 3 to 4 qt warm glass mixing bowl (use a warm bowl... you don't want a cold bowl to take the heat out of the warm water).

> 14 oz warm Water

Add salt and yeast... give a quick stir to combine.

> 1-1/2 tsp Salt
> 1-1/4 tsp Dry Yeast (Instant or Active Dry Yeast)

Add flour... stir until dough forms a shaggy ball, scrape dry flour from side of bowl, then tumble dough to combine moist flour with dry flour.

> 3-1/2 cups Bread Flour

Cover bowl with plastic wrap, place in a warm draft-free location, and proof for 1-1/2 hours.

1-1/2 hours later (mini loaf pans)

When dough has risen and developed its gluten structure... spray 8 mini loaf pans (5-3/4" x 3-1/4" x 2-1/4") with no-stick cooking spray, place in rimmed baking sheet (makes it easier to carry), and set aside.

"Degas, pull and stretch"... stick handle end of a plastic spoon in the dough and stir (dough will form a sticky ball). Then, scrape side of bowl to get remainder of the dough into the sticky dough ball.

"Roll-to-coat"... sprinkle dough ball and side of bowl with flour and roll-to-coat (dusting dough ball with flour will make it easier to handle and shape dough).

> 2 Tbsp Bread Flour

Dust work surface with flour, roll dough (and excess flour) out of bowl onto work surface.

Press lightly to flatten... and divide dough into 8 portions (as you would a pizza). Then (one portion at a time)... roll dough on work surface in flour to shape (adding flour as needed), press to flatten and place in pan (pan will finish shaping rolls for you).

Place rimmed baking sheet in a warm draft-free location, cover with a lint-free towel, and proof for 30 minutes.

Before dough is fully proofed...

Move rack to middle of oven and pre-heat to 450 degrees F.

30 minutes later

When dough has proofed and oven has come to temperature... place rimmed baking sheet in oven and bake for 20 minutes.

20 minutes later

Remove from oven, gently turn rolls out on work surface, and place on cooling rack.

Hamburger Buns (mini round cake pans)

I frequently use store bought hamburger buns, but there are times when I'm looking for something special and a fresh from the oven artisan bun can change a good hamburger into a great dining experience. You'll never find a hamburger bun like these in a grocery store. I used 8 *Wilton* mini round cake pans to shape the rolls.

Option:

Traditional method... if you wish to use the traditional method... decrease yeast from 1-1/4 tsp to 1/4 tsp and proof 8 to 24 hours.

Hamburger Buns

Pour warm water in a 3 to 4 qt warm glass mixing bowl (use a warm bowl... you don't want a cold bowl to take the heat out of the warm water).

    14 oz warm Water

Add salt and yeast... give a quick stir to combine.

    1-1/2 tsp Salt
    1-1/4 tsp Dry Yeast (Instant or Active Dry Yeast)

Add flour... stir until dough forms a shaggy ball, scrape dry flour from side of bowl, then tumble dough to combine moist flour with dry flour.

    3-1/2 cups Bread Flour

Cover bowl with plastic wrap, place in a warm draft-free location, and proof for 1-1/2 hours.

1-1/2 hours later (mini round cake pan)

When dough has risen and developed its gluten structure... spray 8 mini round cake pans (4" x 1-1/4") with no-stick cooking spray, place in rimmed baking sheet (makes it easier to carry them), and set aside.

"Degas, pull and stretch"... stick handle end of a plastic spoon in the dough and stir (dough will form a sticky ball). Then, scrape side of bowl to get remainder of the dough into the sticky dough ball.

"Roll-to-coat"... sprinkle dough ball and side of bowl with flour and roll-to-coat (dusting dough ball with flour will make it easier to handle and shape dough).

    2 Tbsp Bread Flour

Dust work surface with flour, roll dough (and excess flour) out of bowl onto work surface.

Press lightly to flatten... then divide dough into 8 portions (like a pizza) and place one in each pan (pan will shape roll).

Place pans in a warm draft-free location, cover with a lint-free towel, and proof for 30 minutes.

Before dough is fully proofed...

Move rack to middle of oven and pre-heat to 450 degrees F.

30 minutes later

When dough has proofed and oven has come to temperature... put rimmed baking sheet in oven and bake for 20 minutes.

20 minutes later

Remove from oven, gently turn rolls out on work surface, and place on cooling rack.

No-Knead Pizza Dough & Pizza

You'll be pleasantly surprised with how easy it is to make pizza dough. Just mix... wait... and "poof", you have pizza dough. And, once you have pizza dough you can make pizzas, calzones, breadsticks, garlic knots or anything else your little ole' heart desires.

"You better cut the pizza in four pieces because I'm not hungry enough to eat six."

Yogi Berra, Baseball Hall of Fame catcher

No-Knead Pizza Dough

I experimented with a variety of herbs, spices, and pizza dough flavor packs, but found I preferred to add flavors to the pizza toppings instead of the dough, because the flavors I want in a vegetarian pizza are different than the flavors I add to a pepperoni pizza.

Methods & Sizes: I have two methods for making pizza dough, "Traditional" (proofs for 8 to 24 hours), and "Turbo" (proofs for 1-1/2 hours). I also have two sizes… standard (3-1/2 cups flour) & personal (2 cups flour).

Portions: Standard size (3-1/2 cups flour) can be divided into 2 portions for two 16" thin crust pizzas or 4 portions for four thin crust 12" pizzas or four "Perfect Little 9" Pizzas". Personal size (2 cups flour) is intended for one 16" pizza or it can be divided into 2 portions for two 12" thin crust pizzas or two "Perfect Little 9" Pizzas".

Saving: If you wish to save dough… divide into portions (optional), drizzle with olive oil, place in zip-lock bag(s), remove excess air, and refrigerate for up to two days or freeze for up to two months. To thaw dough… move dough from freezer to refrigerator the day before, then place on counter to come to room temperature.

Note: Pizza dough (like all other flatbreads) doesn't need a 2nd proofing… it can be used immediately after shaping.

"Traditional" Pizza Dough... proofs for 8 to 24 hours

The "traditional" method for making no-knead bread is very popular. The same process can be used to make pizza dough. This recipe makes two 16" or four 12" thin crust pizzas.

Pour water into a 3-1/2 to 4 qt glass mixing bowl.
>14 oz cool Water

Add salt, yeast, and olive oil... give a quick stir to combine.
>1-1/2 tsp Salt
>1/4 tsp Dry Yeast (Instant or Active Dry Yeast)
>2 Tbsp extra-virgin Olive Oil

Add flour... stir until dough forms a shaggy ball, scrape dry flour from side of bowl, then tumble dough to combine moist flour with dry flour.
>3-1/2 cups Bread Flour

Cover bowl with plastic wrap, place on counter, and proof for 8 to 24 hours.

8 to 24 hours later

When dough has risen and developed its gluten structure... move rack to the middle of oven and preheat to 450 degrees F.

"Degas, pull and stretch"... stick handle end of a plastic spoon in the dough and stir (dough will form a sticky ball). Then, scrape side of bowl to get remainder of the dough into the sticky dough ball.

"Roll-to-coat"... sprinkle dough ball and side of bowl with flour and roll-to-coat (dusting dough ball with flour will make it easier to handle and shape dough).
>2 Tbsp Bread Flour

Dust work surface with flour, roll dough (and excess flour) out of bowl onto work surface.

Press lightly to flatten, divide dough into 2 portions, and form each portion into a ball for two 16" thin crust pizzas. Or divide dough into 4 portions, and form each portion into a ball for four thin crust 12" pizzas or four "Perfect Little 9" Pizzas".

If you aren't ready to use the pizza dough balls... cover with a lint-free towel to rest.

"Turbo" Pizza Dough... proof for 1-1/2 hours

If you don't want to wait 8 to 24 hours... this is an excellent alterative. This recipe makes two 16" or four 12" thin crust pizzas.

Pour warm water in a 3-1/2 to 4 qt warm glass mixing bowl (use a warm bowl... you don't want a cold bowl to take the heat out of the warm water).
 14 oz warm Water

Add salt, yeast, and olive oil... give a quick stir to combine.
 1-1/2 tsp Salt
 1-1/4 tsp Dry Yeast (Instant or Active Dry Yeast)
 2 Tbsp extra-virgin Olive Oil

Add flour... stir until dough forms a shaggy ball, scrape dry flour from side of bowl, then tumble dough to combine moist flour with dry flour.
 3-1/2 cups Bread Flour

Cover bowl with plastic wrap, place in a warm draft-free location, and proof for 1-1/2 hours.

1-1/2 hours later

When dough has risen and developed its gluten structure... move rack to the middle of oven and preheat to 450 degrees F.

"Degas, pull and stretch"... stick handle end of a plastic spoon in the dough and stir (dough will form a sticky ball). Then, scrape side of bowl to get remainder of the dough into the sticky dough ball.

"Roll-to-coat"... sprinkle dough ball and side of bowl with flour and roll-to-coat (dusting dough ball with flour will make it easier to handle and shape dough).
 2 Tbsp Bread Flour

Dust work surface with flour, roll dough (and excess flour) out of bowl onto work surface.

Press lightly to flatten, divide dough into 2 portions, and form each portion into a ball for two 16" thin crust pizzas. Or divide dough into 4 portions, and form each portion into a ball for four thin crust 12" pizzas or four "Perfect Little 9" Pizzas".

If you aren't ready to use the pizza dough balls... cover with a lint-free towel to rest.

Supporting video: World's Easiest Pizza Dough... ready to bake in less than 2 hours (no-knead "hands-free" technique)... demonstrates "Turbo" method including "hands-free technique" for making the dough.

Personal Size Pizza Dough

The personal size will give you one 16" or two 12" thin crust pizzas.

Pour warm water in a 2-1/2 to 3-1/2 qt warm glass mixing bowl (use a warm bowl... you don't want a cold bowl to take the heat out of the warm water).
>   8 oz warm Water

Add salt, yeast, and olive oil... give a quick stir to combine.
>   1/2 tsp Salt (rounded)
>   1 tsp Dry Yeast (Instant or Active Dry Yeast)
>   1 Tbsp extra-virgin Olive Oil

Add flour... stir until dough forms a shaggy ball, scrape dry flour from side of bowl, then tumble dough to combine moist flour with dry flour.
>   2 cups Bread Flour

Cover bowl with plastic wrap, place in a warm draft-free location, and proof for 1-1/2 hours.

1-1/2 hours later

When dough has risen and developed its gluten structure... move rack to the middle of oven and preheat to 450 degrees F.

"Degas, pull and stretch"... stick handle end of a plastic spoon in the dough and stir (dough will form a sticky ball). Then, scrape side of bowl to get remainder of the dough into the sticky dough ball.

"Roll-to-coat"... sprinkle dough ball and side of bowl with flour and roll-to-coat (dusting dough ball with flour will make it easier to handle and shape dough).
>   2 Tbsp Bread Flour

Dust work surface with flour, roll dough (and excess flour) out of bowl onto work surface.

Press lightly to flatten for one 16" pizza or divide dough into 2 portions, and form each portion into a ball for two thin crust 12" pizzas or two "Perfect Little 9" Pizzas".

If you aren't ready to use the pizza dough balls... cover with a lint-free towel to rest.

Supporting video: <u>World's Easiest Pizza Dough (updated)... no-knead dough... no machines (just a glass bowl and a spoon)</u> demonstrates personal size pizza dough using the traditional method.

Mushroom-Black Olive Pizza

Prep: Move rack to the middle of oven and preheat to 450 degrees F.

Shape: Place dough in the center of work space, press firmly to flatten... then work from the center pushing the dough outward to make a larger disk adding flour as needed.

<u>1 Pizza Dough Ball</u>

Pick disk up by the edge and move your hands along the edge allowing gravity to stretch the dough until it forms a larger circle... then use a pizza roller to finish shaping and place in pizza pan.

Toppings: Spread a thin layer of sauce on the dough, generously sprinkle with cheese, cover with mushrooms, add black olives, and sprinkle with a little more cheese.

<u>3 heaping Tbsp Pizza Sauce</u>
<u>8 oz shredded Provolone-Mozzarella Cheese</u>
<u>6 oz sliced Mushrooms</u>
<u>1/2 cup (2-1/4 oz can) sliced Black Olives</u>

Bake: Put pan in oven and bake for 15 to 18 minutes depending on the thickness of the crust, the toppings, and how you like your cheese.

Serve: Remove from oven, slice and serve.

Meatball & Bacon Pizza
Prep: Move rack to the middle of oven and preheat to 450 degrees F.
Meatballs... place meatballs on a paper plate, microwave on high for 1 minute, cut in half and set aside.
<ins>12 sm frozen Meatballs</ins>
Bacon... trim off excess fat (not all), put paper towel on a paper plate, place bacon in a single layer on one side of the paper towel, fold other side over to cover (prevents splattering), and heat in the microwave on high for 1 to 2 minutes to render the fat, but don't overcook... it's going to be baked.
<ins>4 slices Bacon</ins>
Take bacon out of the microwave, remove paper towel, and allow bacon to cool... then cut bacon into pieces and set aside.
Shape: Place dough in the center of work space, press firmly to flatten... then work from the center pushing the dough outward to make a larger disk adding flour as needed.
<ins>1 Pizza Dough Ball</ins>
Pick disk up by the edge and move your hands along the edge allowing gravity to stretch the dough until it forms a larger circle... then use a pizza roller to finish shaping and place in pizza pan.
Toppings: Spread a thin layer of sauce on dough, generously sprinkle with cheese, and add bacon and meatballs.
<ins>3 heaping Tbsp Pizza Sauce</ins>
<ins>8 oz shredded Provolone-Mozzarella Cheese</ins>
Bake: Put pan in oven and bake for 15 to 18 minutes depending on the thickness of the crust, the toppings, and how you like your cheese.
Serve: Remove from oven, slice and serve.

Note: All meat should be precooked before being added to a pizza.

Perfect Little 9" Cheese Pizza
Prep: Move rack to the middle of oven and preheat to 450 degrees F, drizzle 9" pie pan with olive oil and set aside.
    1 tsp extra-virgin Olive Oil
Shape: Generously dust work surface with flour, place dough ball on work space and roll in flour to coat... then press firmly with the palm of your hand to flatten, use pizza roller to shape into a 9" circle and place in pan.
    1 Pizza Dough Ball
Finish shaping by pressing dough to cover bottom of pan.
Toppings: Spread a thin layer of sauce on dough and generously cover with cheese.
    1 heaping Tbsp Pizza Sauce
    4 oz shredded Provolone-Mozzarella Cheese
Bake: Put pizza in oven and bake for 12 to 15 minutes depending on the thickness of the crust, the toppings, and how you like your cheese.
Serve: Remove from oven, slice and serve.

Perfect Little 9" Mushroom-Black Olive Pizza

Prep: Move rack to the middle of oven and preheat to 450 degrees F, drizzle 9" pie pan with olive oil and set aside.

<u>1 tsp extra-virgin Olive Oil</u>

Shape: Generously dust work surface with flour, place dough ball on work space and roll in flour to coat... then press firmly with the palm of your hand to flatten, use pizza roller to shape into a 9" circle and place in pan.

<u>1 Pizza Dough Ball</u>

Finish shaping by pressing dough to cover bottom of pan.

Toppings: Spread a thin layer of sauce on dough, generously sprinkle with cheese, add mushrooms to cover, add black olives, and sprinkle with a little more cheese.

<u>1 heaping Tbsp Pizza Sauce</u>
<u>4 oz shredded Provolone-Mozzarella Cheese</u>
<u>Mushrooms</u>
<u>Sliced Black Olives</u>

Bake: Put pizza in oven and bake for 12 to 15 minutes depending on the thickness of the crust, the toppings, and how you like your cheese.

Serve: Remove from oven, slice and serve.

Great Galloping Garlic Knots

Prep: Spray an 18" x 13" rimmed baking pan with no-stick spray... and set aside. Combine butter, garlic, herbs and cheese... and set aside.

>   4 Tbsp melted Butter
>   1 heaping tsp Minced Garlic
>   1 tsp Thyme
>   1 tsp Oregano
>   1 tsp grated Parmesan Cheese

Shape: Place dough in the center of work space, press firmly to flatten... then use a pizza roller to shape into a rectangle 12" to 14" wide and 6" to 8" high.

>   1 Pizza Dough Ball

Use a pizza cutter to cut dough into 1" wide strips 6" to 8" long.
Loosely tie strips into knots and place in rimmed baking pan.
Use a measuring spoon (1/4 tsp) to distribute garlic-butter mixture over garlic knots.
Proof: Cover with lint-free towel and proof for 30 minutes.
Prep: Move rack to the middle of oven and preheat to 400 degrees F.
Bake: Slide pan into oven and bake for 20 minutes.
Garnish & Serve: Remove garlic knots from oven, warm garlic-butter mixture in microwave, brush garlic knots with mixture and serve warm.

Notes: I like to add 1 heaping teaspoon minced garlic to the dough when making garlic knots.

Made in the USA
Middletown, DE
14 December 2023

45703554R00053